WHEN COUNTING TO 10 ISN'T ENOUGH

When Counting to 10

Isn't Enough

Defusing Anger

Kathy Collard Miller

Harold Shaw Publishers
Wheaton, Illinois

All Scripture quotations, unless otherwise indicated, are taken from the *New American Standard Bible,* © 1960, 1962, 1963, 1968, 1971, 1973, 1975, 1977 by The Lockman Foundation. Used by permission.

Scripture quotations marked TLB are from *The Living Bible* © 1971. Used by permission of Tyndale House Publishers, Inc., Wheaton, IL 60189. All rights reserved.

Edited by Joan Guest and Esther Waldrop
Cover design by David LaPlaca

ISBN 0-87788-745-4

Library of Congress Cataloging-in-Publication Data

Miller, Kathy C. (Kathy Collard), 1949-
    When counting to 10 isn't enough : defusing anger (help for parents) / Kathy Collard Miller.
        p.   cm.
    ISBN 0-87788-745-4
    1. Anger—Religious aspects—Christianity. 2. Parenting—Religious aspects—Christianity. 3. Child rearing—Religious aspects—Christianity. 4. Miller, Kathy C. (Kathy Collard), 1949-   . I. Title.
    BV4627.8'45—dc20
                                                                    96-3838
                                                                    CIP

02   01   00   99   98   97   96

10   9   8   7   6   5   4   3   2   1

Contents

1

Where Are the Simple Joys of Parenthood?

Two-year-old, blonde-headed Darcy splashed in the bathtub amid suds and toys.

"Time to wash your hair," I announced.

"No, no, Mommy. No wash hair. Please," Darcy pleaded as she shook her thin strands of hair.

"Oh, yes, it's all sticky. It'll feel good to get it nice and clean," I coaxed.

Darcy broke into tears as I rubbed the shampoo into her hair. Suddenly she began rubbing her eyes and yelling, "It's in my eyes. It hurts! It hurts!"

"Oh, it is not," I responded. "There are no suds near your eyes. Besides, it's baby shampoo—it doesn't sting."

She screamed louder.

Suddenly I was overwhelmed with exhaustion. The pressures that had been mounting throughout the day overwhelmed me, and I felt weak. The room seemed to close in on me. The dampness and heat made my clothes stick to my skin. Pushing limp hair away from my forehead and gritting my teeth, I hissed back, "Darcy, there's no shampoo in your eyes. Now hold still or you're in big trouble! Hold still, I said!"

Shrieking, my little girl clawed at her eyes. I turned on the faucet and jerked her to it, pushing her whole head under the running water. Soap flowed down over her face into the tub. She sputtered and coughed, but I didn't care. She was going to get clean whether she liked it or not.

I hurriedly turned off the water. Grabbing her arm, I yanked her out of the tub. Darcy stood shivering and crying. I screamed at her again and again. "The next time you'll hold still when I tell you. We'll do it the way I say, and that's that."

I felt like an erupting volcano of hate. Anger and frustration boiled inside me like hot lava. At that moment I felt like I wanted to kill her.

Spanking her with my hand, I found an outlet for my tension and exhaustion. But spanking became uncontrolled beating, until Darcy's hysterical shrieking brought me back to reason. I carried her into her room and dropped her into bed. Slamming the door behind me, I bolted down the hall, sobbing.

"Oh, Lord Jesus," I gasped. "I hurt Darcy again. I keep saying I won't do it anymore, but I can't control my anger. What's wrong with me?"

I knelt beside my bed and cried for a long time. Darcy's muffled cries reached me, suffocating me in a blanket of guilt.

My thoughts hurled through my mind like hailstones in a storm. *I've been a Christian for ten years; how can I be so angry? I lead a Bible study, and other people think I'm such a strong Christian; how can I be acting like this?*

I wanted to scream, "Help me! Help me!" but I was ashamed and frightened. What if they took my kids away from me? What if everyone knew I abused my child?

I'm not a child abuser! I defended myself. *Or am I?*

"I'm still hurting her," I cried out. "I'm abusing my own child. Oh, God, no!"

The word *abusing* echoed through my mind like a boulder thudding down a canyon wall—strong and final.

There was no hope. I had prayed. I had cried. I had begged for deliverance. If only Larry didn't have to work at night, he could relieve some of the pressure, I thought. Yet I knew that was a hollow hope, since even when he was home, he wasn't emotionally there. How I hated him for his insensitivity! No wonder so many policemen were divorced. Larry seemed to be just like the men he worked with.

How long can I continue like this without seriously injuring Darcy or baby Mark? Darcy's frightened face flashed before me, wrenching my heart like a tree being uprooted by the wind. *I don't want to hurt them. I love them. I want to be the best mother in the world. But I'm so far from that.*

"Oh, Father," I whimpered. "Help me! You've got to. I can't help myself!"

I turned my attention to Darcy and couldn't hear her crying anymore. Walking quietly to her room, I opened the door and peeked in. Her naked body was huddled by the pillow. She saw me and started crying again. Pushing aside my shame, I pulled her pajamas out of her drawer and started to dress her. Her body grew tense at my touch.

"Don't be afraid, Darcy," I said. "I'm not mad at you anymore. Mommy was wrong to hurt you. I'm sorry. I wish I could promise you I'll never get angry with you again—but I can't. Oh, how I wish I could." My tears plopped onto the sheets beside her. I gently tucked her into bed and left the room.

As I put on my nightgown, I wondered if God cared, or if he had deserted me. But deep down, I knew better. I knew that God was always there. *Then where is the help I need?* I wanted to shout. But I pushed the doubt out of my mind as I cried myself to sleep.

Lord, I Want an Instantaneous Deliverance

The next few days I was able to keep my anger in check, but eventually it erupted again. I was convinced I'd never have victory. I concluded that God had given up on me, as each prayer for help seemed to bounce back at me from the ceiling. Over time, I had pushed Darcy down onto the floor, kicked her, and choked her. I worried if I might kill her in my next outburst. There didn't seem to be any hope.

One day after I had lost control again, I remembered Larry had left his off-duty service revolver in the top dresser drawer. As if it were calling to me, it seemed to say, "Kathy, take your life. If you don't, you'll kill Darcy in your next rage."

I started to open the dresser drawer, but then another idea bolted into my mind: *What would people think of Jesus if they heard that Kathy Miller committed suicide?* I prayed, "Lord Jesus, I don't want anyone to think poorly of you. The women in my Bible study group and at church might think no one can help them if I take my life. But that's the very reason I haven't told anyone about my problem. I don't want them to think you aren't strong enough to help anyone with their problems. But why aren't you helping me?"

Somehow I didn't use that gun that day, but I still didn't have any hope. I tried subtly sharing my problem with one friend, but she reacted with shock and condemnation. *Didn't anyone else experience anger toward their children?* I wondered. I was convinced I was the only one—especially the only Christian!

As I continued to pray for an instant deliverance from my anger, I believed God was obviously answering no to my prayer. What I didn't realize then is that, yes, he wanted to free me, but not instantaneously. Instead, he began to show me the underlying causes of my anger and, through a process of growth that took almost a year, gave me the solutions for it.

I first experienced a glimmer of hope when I shared my struggle with one of the women from the neighborhood Bible study I taught, and she didn't condemn me as my other friend had. Then I began reading books about disciplining children effectively and coping with frustration. I also asked the women of the Bible study to pray for me. I saw the truth of James 5:16 make a difference: "Therefore, confess your sins to one another, and pray for one another, so that you may be healed. The effective prayer of a righteous man can accomplish much."

Little by little, I grew more patient with Darcy. God was showing himself faithful. He did love me after all, and he cared about our family. I was thrilled and over time grew more confident that God did have a plan for me to be a loving mother. In time, he even healed the relationship between Larry and me through a couples' retreat we attended. Eventually I knew that God had indeed delivered me from being an abusive mother.

This book isn't only for child abusers, but for anyone who struggles with anger—and isn't that all of us to some degree? In the following pages, I will share with you many of the insights and truths God taught me during my difficult time. I'll also reveal other principles for defusing anger that I've gleaned over many years of teaching parenting classes and seminars. I trust this little book will give you hope and help— hope to know God cares about you, whether you fear you're actually abusing your child or not, and practical help to give you confidence in knowing you can be the loving parent you want to be.

2

No One Plans to Be an Angry Parent

No one starts out as a parent planning to abuse or even to be angry with their child. I had every intention of being the perfect parent. In fact, I wholeheartedly believed that if I were to ever yell at my child, it would destroy his or her self-esteem. Having been raised in a family where children and family were highly esteemed, I grew up believing that the most fulfilling thing I could do would be to grow up, get married, and have children.

When Larry and I were married in 1970, I knew that I was on my way to fulfilling that wonderful dream of motherhood. After a reasonable time, we decided it was time to start our family. We were established in a home, Larry had a secure job as a policeman and real estate agent, and we knew we could afford for me to quit my job. Everything seemed perfect . . . until I couldn't get pregnant. Month after disappointing month went by. I began to wonder if God were playing a cruel joke on me. "Lord, you know how much I want a baby. Please don't wait too long!"

At first I was patient. I knew God must have a reason for his timing, and I could wait. But after a year of waiting, my main prayer concern was getting pregnant. "Lord, I just can't believe it's not your will for me to be a mother. I must be a mother." I didn't say it, but my attitude cried out, *I can't be fulfilled unless I have a baby!* My whole focus became concentrated on becoming pregnant. Several times I thought I'd seen signs in my body that meant I was pregnant. One time we even announced to my family we were going to have a baby, but every hint of pregnancy became a disappointment.

Another year passed. I was frantic. Not only did I want the fulfillment of being a mother, I also hated my job and knew Larry didn't want me to quit without a good enough reason—like a baby. I so wanted a baby to love and to love me back. "Please, Lord, you must grant me this request. I'll do anything!" I bargained.

In time a rash developed on my right hand, and I knew it was caused by my nervousness about getting pregnant. I tried to trust God and relax about his will for me, but certainly he couldn't be serious about me not having a baby. I kept praying, "God, I really want to trust you. If it's not the best for me to ever be a mother, I'll try to believe you know best. I surrender to your plan." But just as soon as the words of surrender were spoken, I yanked them back as if they were attached to a rubber band. I had to have a baby.

One morning as I opened my devotional book, it focused on Psalm 113. When I came to verse 9, my heart started pounding with expectation. It read, "He makes the barren woman abide in her house as a joyful mother of children." *God, are you trying to tell me something?* I prayed. *I have seen some changes in my body that could be pregnancy and my period's late, but I've seen those hints before and I wasn't.*

God didn't seem to answer. I didn't think I could handle another false alarm to raise and then dash my hopes. Later that day as I vacuumed my living room carpet, I thought about that devotion's emphasis on Psalm 113 and hope swelled again within me. I looked down at my stomach and whispered, "I don't know if anyone's in there, but if you are, I love you."

Two weeks later, my pregnancy was confirmed. I was thrilled! I was finally going to be a mother. I was finally going to be fulfilled. My dreams were going to be realized after so long. By the time Darcy was born in October 1974, we'd been married more than four years.

Unfortunately, I was completely unaware of the seeds of anger and abuse that eventually sprouted into uncontrolled rage. Looking back, I can pinpoint the warning signs.

Warning Sign #1: Unrealistic Expectations

First, *my desire to be the perfect mother set up unrealistic expectations.* If I was less than perfect, I believed my child couldn't grow up emotionally healthy, nor would he or she want to become a Christian. I believed that yelling at a child would destroy his or her self-esteem. Now I know that every parent experiences frustration, and that it shouldn't be denied or ignored but dealt with constructively.

I remember one of the first times I became totally frustrated with Darcy. She was less than a year old and wouldn't go to sleep for her nap. The longer she resisted my efforts to make her sleep, the angrier I became. I needed her to take her nap, and she wasn't cooperating! Finally, at the end of my emotional rope, I dropped her into her crib crying and ran out of her room, slamming the door behind me.

She cried and cried. I could picture her puckered face with tears running down her cheeks. But I couldn't handle being around her right then, so I let her cry as I tried to keep busy in another part of the house. Eventually I noticed that she'd stopped crying. I peeked into her room and found her asleep in her crib, tears still wetting her cheeks.

Oh, no, I thought, as I tiptoed out of the room again. *She's going to hate me when she wakes up. I'm a terrible mother! She'll never forgive me for making her cry herself to sleep. She usually is so eager to see me after her nap, but I bet she won't even want me around her this time.* During the two hours that she slept, I worried constantly that my relationship with my precious baby was destroyed and that she would hate me the rest of her life.

Later that afternoon, I thought I heard sounds coming from her bedroom. *Well, this is it,* I told myself as my heart pounded in fear, wondering how she would respond when she saw me. I slowly opened the door and peeked in. She was sitting in her crib, patting her blanket. I opened the door wider, and as soon as she saw me, she jumped up, flung out her arms to be picked up, and giggled in delight, "Mama." A huge smile lit up her face.

She still loves me, I thought in amazement. I couldn't believe it. It was as if she didn't even remember how mad I had been, or that I had made her cry herself to sleep. That day I experienced a hint of a truth: a limited amount of frustration with our children is normal and won't destroy their self-esteem or our relationship with them.

Warning Sign #2: A Need to Be Loved

Another incorrect perspective about motherhood bore the seeds that would sprout into abusive anger later on: *I thought I needed to have a baby in order to be loved.* I thought it was completely normal and healthy to want to have a baby for its love value. I looked forward to having my child show me love. As the previous experience demonstrates, I believed Darcy would stop loving me if I didn't perform well as a mother.

But such a mind-set showed my own low self-esteem. I needed a baby to love me to feel good about myself. This meant trouble when Darcy often demanded more love from me than I possessed, and when she didn't give love in return as often as my needy self-image required. When I needed to discipline Darcy for disobedience or had to tell her "no," I hesitated for fear that she would get angry with me and stop loving me. In trying to avoid making her angry, I became inconsistent in disciplining her. But my inconsistency only caused her frustration, and her temper tantrums became more frequent.

Warning Sign #3: Expectations of Fulfillment

A third seed of my expectations sprouted into anger when *I rarely experienced the fulfillment I had anticipated in my dreams of being a mother.* I still don't know what kind of "fulfillment" I expected during that time, but it didn't surface while changing dirty diapers or training pants, hearing a toddler scream and pound the floor in a temper tantrum, or cleaning up spilled milk at least fourteen times a day. This was fulfillment? Why did I ever even want a baby? I often wondered. Darcy had been an ideal baby, cooperative and vivacious. But as she moved into toddlerhood it seemed she rarely smiled, much less appreciated my efforts to be such a perfect mother—which I failed at miserably.

These seeds of anger began to sprout and grow, and I was unaware of the destruction they would cause in the future. Since then I've learned that my reactions are common among those who become extremely aggravated with their children.

And often that aggravation does lead to child abuse. Many years ago when I thought of a child abuser, I envisioned a parent who woke up planning how they would hurt their child that day. Most people identify abuse with extreme forms of punishment or physical harm. Now I know that most abusers want to be good parents, but because of many different factors, they are overwhelmed and take it out on their child.

Defining Child Abuse

Parents Anonymous, a self-help organization offering group assistance, identifies six different types of abuse:

1. *Physical abuse:* any injury that is not accidental.
2. *Physical neglect:* lack of proper food, clothing, medical care, parental guidance, or supervision.
3. *Sexual abuse:* performing sexual acts with a child, or knowing it is happening, but not taking action to stop it.
4. *Verbal abuse:* using insulting, coarse, or bad language; scolding harshly or reviling.
5. *Emotional abuse:* providing a negative emotional atmosphere, making the child feel inadequate, inferior, or unimportant.
6. *Emotional neglect:* giving neither negative or positive attention; not showing any feelings toward the child.

The United States Congress defines child abuse as "the physical or mental injury, sexual abuse, negligent treatment or maltreatment of a child under the age of 18 by a person who is responsible for the child's welfare." We don't often think of neglect, verbal lashings, or "putting a child down" as child abuse, but they are.

Some Statistics and Vital Information

National child abuse expert Jim Reid is the founder and director of For Kid's Sake, a national organization that helps to prevent child abuse. He offers us the following interesting statistics and information about child abuse. Like myself, *virtually all child abusers have low self-esteem, and many have troubled marriages.* They are generally socially isolated, with little support from their families, and they rarely get away from their children. They may resent the fact that another person's demands and care disrupts their own lives.

Child abusers tend to be depressed, lonely, or fearful. They usually feel inadequate in their parenting role and know little about child development. Parents are more susceptible during a rapid series of changes or crises. Also, many abusers are victims of a slight neurological impairment, which may not be detected by others, but which lowers their frustration tolerance.

Jim Reid's research shows that *a child's crying is the behavior that most often triggers child abuse.* The parent may interpret the crying as "You aren't meeting my needs—you are not a good parent." As a result, an insecure mother or father feels overwhelmed with frustration. This frustration is then translated into hostility, which is expressed in abusive behavior toward the one who appears to have caused it.

The second most common trigger of child abuse is toilet training. I can certainly comprehend the tensions around that trigger. Of course, any tension should not send us into abusive reactions, but if anything will do it, trying to toilet train an uncooperative child will.

I well remember my own frustrations regarding Darcy's unwillingness to cooperate with my plans for toilet training. I was determined to not have two children in diapers, and she was just as determined to have dirty, wet training pants. Darcy might not walk down the aisle at her wedding wearing training pants, but I was terrified she would go to kindergarten wearing them!

Each time she had an accident, I was overwhelmed with feelings of failure. Each time Darcy didn't obey me, I judged myself inadequate. Why couldn't I produce a trained child? Plus, I just knew she must be giving me all this trouble on purpose. She must be trying to communicate that she thought I was a terrible mother, and I had to agree with her. That made my feelings of inadequacy and low self-esteem grow even more.

During my steps of healing, I finally put her back into diapers, realizing that she really wasn't ready. Several months later, when I was no longer controlled by anger and able to separate my own identity from hers, we tried again and she quickly became potty trained. I'm now convinced that we try to toilet train our children before they're capable of performing and then we blame ourselves. I think it's much wiser to hold off and risk the cutting remarks of others than to put ourselves into a position of becoming angry and diminishing a good relationship with our child.

The average age of child abusers is twenty-six. This was again similar to my experience; I was twenty-seven. But this statistic really surprised me. I thought that the average age might be eighteen or twenty-one. After all, wouldn't it be the young mothers with seemingly little life experience and maturity who might falter in their parenting skills? As a slightly older mother, I believed that my "advanced" maturity would give me the ability to be a great mother.

In retrospect, I can see that being older may have just set up higher expectations of myself and others. Plus, now that

I'm in my forties, I can see that I really didn't know very much at all! Yet at the time I felt experienced in life and how to love others. Such immature thinking contributed to my inability to handle life's struggles. Of course, none of us can be experienced parents until we actually do it. So regardless of our age, we learn as we go along.

Another statistic that isn't so surprising is the fact that *the majority of battered children are two years old.* The "terrible twos" stage is a tough one. Often another child comes along to make the family feel even more stressed, and as a result life becomes overwhelming.

At the time that life was overbearing for me, I was surprised that I didn't take my anger out on my infant son as I did on Darcy. Since then I've learned that most often, only one child is abused in the family. I've talked to many other struggling parents who are also surprised that their anger is expressed primarily toward one child. Yet this reaction seems quite common.

One cause of this behavior may be that the child may resemble a person with whom the abuser is upset. To me, my daughter physically resembled my husband, Larry. Emotionally, I felt that I couldn't make him obey me, and I couldn't make her obey me either.

Another cause could be that the child has a similar personality and temperament to that of the abusive parent. This might bring up painful memories of his or her own childhood, which may also have been abusive. A parent usually responds to a child in the same way that he or she was once treated by their own abusive parent, thus creating greater frustration. "I don't want to treat my child as I was treated, yet I seem powerless to stop. What's wrong with me?" they reason.

Subtle Influences in the Cycle of Child Abuse

Most people do not understand or comprehend the intense cycle that child abuse creates. Abused children grow up determined to be everything good that their parents weren't. Yet the fact that they judge their parents' failures only creates a foundation of bitterness and resentment that offers them a lack of grace in their own parenting role. Grace can be defined as the favor and goodness offered to someone even when they don't deserve it.

When we understand that by offering our parents forgiveness—and thus grace—we will actually lay a foundation for forgiving ourselves when we are imperfect parents. Grace extended to ourselves gives strength to keep trying, rather than condemning ourselves, giving up, and feeling that God has given up on us.

Although I was not abused as a child, I did learn wrong attitudes about dealing with anger from my mother's frustrations with life. Once I became a mother, I could learn to forgive her because I better understood the stresses that motherhood brings. She did the best she could and overcame many obstacles to offer me love and support. I have a choice: I can focus on the ways she didn't meet my needs, or I can focus on the ways she lived up to my expectations. Just as I'm learning to focus on the positive, I hope my own children learn to do the same.

Unfortunately, *societal attitudes subtly contribute to the potential for child abuse.* One detrimental attitude is that being a mother is no longer a valued profession. Public opinion subtly tells women they are wasting their time by being "just" housewives and homemakers. In many people's eyes, they are misusing skills that could be better used to "contribute" to society. The hostile environment of such secular attitudes can generate frustration in mothers. They can be led to believe that others judge them as a "drain on society."

In addition, *idealistic dreams about the "joys of parenthood" supply fuel for new parents' expectations.* Few of us are prepared for the change in lifestyle that parenthood ushers in. We soon learn that although being a parent is a joy, it also brings a hefty portion of physical and emotional exhaustion and tedium.

Another subtle influence on the problem of child abuse is our *society's acceptance and approval of abortion.* A parent may subconsciously reason that if another person can legally kill a baby a few months before birth, what is so bad about roughing up a child a little afterward, especially if you don't kill him?

Are You Over the Line?

There are many causes of child abuse, and at times any parent can wonder whether he or she is about to step over the line from normal parental frustration to child abuse. If you feel you are close to that line and desire help to cope with your anger, here are ten questions to help you decide. (These have been developed by the ministry of For Kid's Sake, 29280 Central Ave. Suite G., Lake Elsinore, CA 92532, 1-800-898-4KID).

1. Do you feel inadequate as a parent and about your knowledge of child development?
2. Do you have low self-esteem?
3. Are you getting angry more frequently?
4. Have some people indicated your disciplinary reactions are unreasonable?
5. Do you feel your child seldom meets your expectations or wonder if your expectations are too high?

6. Do you feel isolated or depressed?
7. Have you left a mark on your child?
8. Were you abused as a child?
9. Do you envision any sexual fantasies about your child?
10. Do you visualize hurting your child and think it would feel good to do so?

A check mark by one or two of these questions doesn't necessarily mean your anger is out of control. *But if you checked more than two, or if you checked any of the last four questions, it's imperative that you get help.* Your anger is most likely not going to improve on its own without your working through some of the issues that cause it. Please don't be like I was. I kept thinking I would never get angry again, but I did. Now I believe my anger would have been healed sooner if I had sought professional counseling.

Let God guide you to the person who will be able to respond to you in the best way. A Christian counselor can usually be relied upon as a good first step. Another possibility would be a group like Parents Anonymous. (You can usually find a group in your area through your telephone directory.)

Please get the help that will assist you to become the loving, patient parent you want to be. You won't regret it. You may even wonder, after the healing begins, why you waited so long.

3

What Is Anger?

Mark's hungry cries startled me out of a deep sleep. The sun's rays barely permeated the overcast sky; the high clouds made it seem more like a summer morning than one in the middle of May. Dragging myself out of bed, I wondered why I was still so weary. Even after ten hours of sleep, my body felt as though I had just run a marathon.

Plodding through the morning routine, I suspected I was coming down with a cold, but I didn't feel congested. I comforted myself with the promise of a nap.

Later, Mark went down for his nap easily, but Darcy wouldn't settle down in her room. As I lay down on my bed and started to relax, Darcy wandered into my room, her thin blonde hair damply matted against her head.

"Darcy, you're supposed to be in bed sleeping. Now go back to your room."

"Mommy, me not tired. Can I color, please?" Her bright, alert eyes convinced me she really wasn't sleepy.

"Oh, all right. You can color here on the floor while I rest." A warning bell in my brain signaled potential danger, but I assured myself that I would keep an eye on her while I rested.

I got up, found the crayons and coloring book, and spread them out on the carpet beside my bed. Then I strictly cautioned her, "Now remember, Darcy, you color only on the paper and nothing else, okay?"

Her happy face anticipated coloring in her new Lassie coloring book. I smiled, lay back down on the bed, and watched her scribble on the first page.

Oh, this feels so good. My muscles relaxed, and as I closed my eyes I felt peaceful, more peaceful than I had felt in the last couple of weeks. *This feels too good to be true.*

Suddenly I sat up straight. I realized that I had drifted off to sleep and had completely lost track of time—and Darcy. I looked around the room. Half of the crayons were scattered about the floor, and the closet door featured an assortment of red crayon circles.

"Darcy! Where are you?" I implored. *Oh, no! All the walls will be crayoned.* As I felt a burning flash of anger sear through my body, I wondered whether I was more angry with Darcy or myself. I ran down the hall, following the crayon-marked walls. Turning the corner to her room, I stared in disbelief as Darcy sat on her bed, drawing on the wallpaper.

"Darcy! You brat—look what you've done! How am I ever going to get all these marks off so Larry won't know what happened?" I grabbed Darcy by the shoulders and lifted her into the air. Face to face I screamed, "Darcy, I told you not to color on the walls. Why won't you behave? Can't you do anything right?"

I shook her. Her head wobbled back and forth as she looked at me in wide-eyed horror. "Brat, brat, brat! Sometimes I hate you." In my mind's eye, I imagined hurling her onto the floor, her body landing with a dull thud. I wanted to hurt her. A second later, the reality of my thoughts gripped me, and I laid her on the bed. "Oh, God," I sobbed. "I really could have hurt her. I don't hate her. I hate myself. What am I going to do?"

I threw my arms around Darcy's trembling, whimpering body and hugged her tight. "I'm sorry. I'm sorry. It was my fault you colored on the walls." I coaxed her into my arms and gently rocked back and forth. "Why am I so irritable and angry, Darcy? I just don't understand it."

As Darcy cried softly, I surveyed all the bad times I had had during the last couple of weeks. It seemed as though I was always trying to figure out why I was so angry. In the beginning I got few answers, but as time went along, God revealed more truth about my situation. In time, through that process of growth, the Lord strengthened me and pulled me up out of my pit of despair.

Some Reasons for Anger

As I struggled in my despair, I often wondered why God gave human beings this strong emotion of anger anyway. Didn't he know it would get us into a lot of trouble? After some time of working through my own anger, I came to believe that the primary reason we have the ability to get angry is because God made us in his image, and he experiences holy anger and judgment.

Another reason we have the ability to get angry is because anger can help us survive. Anger, like other emotions, generates energy. In the case of anger, that energy can give us extra motivation to struggle to live. Jesus exhibited righteous anger at the unrighteousness around him. I suspect that another one of God's reasons for giving us the ability to get angry was so that we would use that energy to right the wrongs around us.

Recently I received a fund-raising letter from a Christian organization. As I read through it, I was fascinated by its unique way of communicating its message. The first line of the letter read, "This letter will make you angry." Then several times throughout the letter they asked, "Doesn't that make you angry?" This organization needed money to fight unrighteousness in the world, and they were trying to make the readers angry enough to do something about it.

As I pondered this technique, I realized that many Christians, myself included, grow quickly apathetic about fundraising letters and pleas for money. The people involved in sending this letter knew that and wanted to create the tension and energy necessary to provoke an active response. There's the key. Anger creates tension, and tension can create energy— energy to pull any of us out of our apathy.

The dictionary defines anger as a "strong feeling of displeasure." Anger is an emotional reaction to a wrong that has been done, or it can be caused by disappointment that something good we hoped for did not materialize. In my parenting seminars, parents have defined anger as rage, a blazing flame, intense frustration, violent wrath, and other anguished feelings. Although anger has many causes, such as being misunderstood and having one's feelings hurt, more than 95 percent of mothers surveyed attributed their anger to frustration. Such frustration may stem from having a goal or desire blocked, not getting enough done, facing deadlines, or a host of other problems.

Sometimes, rather than honestly communicating our anger, we hide it behind other reactions and don't recognize it for what it is. We might say we're aggravated, upset, cross, or annoyed. Somehow those words don't sound as bad as *angry*. We sometimes try to disguise it, knowing that many people, especially Christians, mistakenly believe that anger is always sinful. Those people usually equate anger with "losing control," and thus brand all anger as wrong. But people do get angry *without* losing control, and that's not wrong.

Are Angry Feelings Sinful?

My generation grew up thinking we weren't supposed to get angry. Anger was an unpleasant emotion that wasn't acceptable in public; it wasn't respectable. So like many others, I tried to push my angry feelings back down inside of me.

It wasn't until a few years ago that I learned the difference between feeling angry and having a pervasive attitude of anger. A *feeling* is that first flash of emotion within us, over which we have no control. It wells up within us before we even realize it's there. For instance, if your best friend came up to you and hit you in the face, you most likely would feel angry. No matter how much you might love that person and want to understand why he or she did that, you still will react emotionally. That is a feeling.

These first flash feelings, our emotions, were built into us by God and are neither right nor wrong. They have no moral quality in themselves because they are not something we can control. Some of our emotions are pleasant, such as happiness, joy, or calmness, and some are unpleasant, such as anger, fear, sadness, and irritation. But they are not right or wrong.

An *attitude* is what we decide to do with a feeling once it emerges. It involves a conscious choice, which leads to our actions. We usually don't have too much trouble letting pleasant feelings turn into proper attitudes. That's easy. Feeling happy can become an attitude of cheerfulness, joy, or generosity. But with an unpleasant feeling, we have a more difficult choice of whether to turn it into a godly or an unrighteous attitude.

This chart will help clarify this difference:

A Feeling	*An Attitude*
—has no morality	—is moral
—is an unconscious, spontaneous reaction	—is a conscious choice
—is an emotion given to us by God	—is a decision I make about what I will do with my feeling
—is pleasant or unpleasant	—is right or wrong

Once we experience that first flash feeling of anger, we can choose to let it turn into an ungodly attitude of bitterness, resentment, or hate, or into an attitude of love, forgiveness, and trusting God. If we consistently choose to allow angry feelings to become angry attitudes, we quickly get caught in a habit or pattern of anger. The more we travel this downward spiral, the harder it is to choose godly reactions of love.

This same point is made by the apostle Paul in Ephesians 4:26-27: "If you are angry, don't sin by nursing your grudge. Don't let the sun go down with you still angry—get over it quickly; for when you are angry, you give a mighty foothold to the devil" (TLB). These verses acknowledge that we are going to get angry (and that's not wrong). They then tell us we should not let that anger become sin—let it turn into an attitude by neglecting to face it. We should not ignore it or say we don't feel angry.

"Don't sin by nursing your grudge" reminds us that anger can become sin if we let it continue without dealing with it—if we allow ourselves to enjoy being angry. Isn't it true that it sometimes feels good to wallow in anger? Instead, God wants us to handle it quickly, and not let it eat away inside of us.

"Don't let the sun go down with you still angry," Ephesians 4:26 directs. What a good guideline! Our angry feeling wouldn't have time to turn into a negative attitude or habit if we followed that command. If we all resolved our anger before sunset, we wouldn't go to bed angry with our spouse or wake up and lash out at our children. We wouldn't give our anger a chance to turn into bitterness, or resentment . . . or an ulcer.

Christian psychologist David Augsburger explains it this way: "Anger is a vital, valid, natural emotion. As an emotion, it is in itself neither right nor wrong. The rightness or wrongness depends on the way it is released and exercised."[1]

Don't Push It Down

Why is it necessary and important to understand the difference between feelings and attitudes? Because if we believe all anger is sinful, as soon as we feel angry, we think we've sinned. Then we condemn ourselves and try to squelch the feeling. We tell ourselves we aren't really angry because it's wrong to feel that way. As a result we become even angrier. As one young mother said, "I get angry with myself for being angry!"

I didn't realize it at the time, but my attitude about anger became fixed in my mind and heart because of an incident in the third grade. For a reason I've since forgotten, I became enraged with my best friend, Irene, who lived across the street. In a moment of carelessness I punched her in the nose. As Irene ran across the street, screaming in surprise and pain, I stood paralyzed. I couldn't believe I'd done such a horrible thing! I berated myself: *See what happens when you get angry. You had better never get angry again!*

Although I later apologized to Irene and she forgave me, the attitude about anger that was solidified within me would affect me for many years. For from that point on, my goal was to never get angry again. With such an unrealistic goal, I continually failed—and more important, I constantly tried to suppress my angry feelings. But all they did was get buried alive. My self-condemnation had begun a downward-spiral cycle that was broken only when God healed me from being a child abuser.

When we condemn ourselves for feeling angry (something we can't prevent in the first place), we push it deep within us, where it builds up with anger from other situations. We think ignoring it will cause it to go away. In reality, when we bury our live anger, it boils inside us until we release it in an emotional outburst, like a teakettle with greater and greater steam. Then we wonder where all that anger came from.

If we would instead recognize our feelings of anger for what they are—part of our humanness—and not try to shove them away, we could deal with them effectively. By realizing that the *feelings of anger* are not sin, we can accept ourselves as we truly are: human beings with feelings. Then we can control our anger. Dr. Theodore Isaac Rubin observes:

> Our feelings control us when we subvert them and are no longer aware they exist. They then have an autonomy of their own. When we know what we feel, when our feelings are integrated as parts of the whole of us, then regardless of their intensity, we remain completely in charge of ourselves and of all our feelings—as part of a central autonomy.
>
> Acceptance, real acceptance of angry feelings, without harsh judgment or moral equivocation, combined with *the ability to express* the anger, will then make possible a choice regarding its expression.[2]

Three Reactions to Anger

Sharon, a twenty-eight-year-old mother of preschoolers, grew up in a Christian home. Her father was a minister and often told Sharon, who was strong-willed: "It's wrong to be angry." "Control yourself; some of our congregation might hear you." Or "Only God can have righteous anger."

She matured into adulthood trying to squelch every feeling of anger and condemning herself when she experienced "unspiritual" emotions. When one of her children disobeyed early in the day, she crammed down her feeling of anger inside her. As the day progressed, more childish disobedience and other problems and pressures caused her to push more and more anger below the surface. By the end of the day she felt like a volcano ready to erupt. Often she exploded when something upsetting occurred in the evening, such as her husband being late for dinner.

Sharon asked for help from a Christian friend who is a psychologist. When he explained the difference between the feeling and attitude of anger, she had difficulty believing he was correct. But when he showed her the biblical teaching in Ephesians 4:26-27, she had to agree with him. Then he explained to her that when she feels angry, she has a choice of three reactions. She can deny, direct, or declare her anger.

Denying our anger is the most destructive choice we can make when we experience that first flash feeling of anger. Denying means that we refuse to accept that we're angry. It's when we say, "Who, me? Angry? I am not! I never get angry. I'm just irritated and frustrated!" The truth is, everyone gets angry at some point in time, but most people don't know how to express it in a healthy way. Unfortunately, as John Powell says, "When I repress my emotions, my stomach keeps score."[3]

When we deny anger, we bottle it up inside of us. Then, at an inappropriate time, we explode, spraying the shattered glass of anger all around us, injuring our relationships with others. Dr. H. Norman Wright says, "Getting angry is not necessarily a sin, but repression of anger is always a sin."[4] That's what Sharon, and I, was experiencing. Fortunately, she is beginning to accept her feelings of anger and realize that denial is not a healthy or godly way to deal with anger. As a result, she can control herself more often. I had to find the same key to deliverance.

Our second choice is *directing our anger.* This means we are aware of our anger and we try to control it by doing something physical. Earlier, we said that anger generates energy. If you've never noticed this energy, the next time you're angry, take note of whether or not your body is physically tense and keyed up. Many women have told me that when they are angry, they want to hit or throw or bang something. That's energy!

When we direct our anger, we realize we're angry and then put the resulting energy into some action. Maybe we scrub the floor or furiously push the vacuum back and forth. Directing it can be good in itself, but unless we discover the real reason for our anger and deal with it, we will not solve the underlying problem, and the pent-up anger will continue to control us. Therefore, the best way to respond to our anger is to combine directing it with the third choice: declaring our anger.

Declaring our anger means communicating our feelings in such a way that the other people involved can receive and accept them. If we rant and rave, accuse and blame, then we'll only make others uncooperative and angry, even if we feel better. By declaring our anger in a healthy way, we'll be in control and influence others positively.

Later we'll talk more about how to declare our anger constructively through a five-step process. Before then, we'll be looking at some other causes of anger. An important one is perfectionism, the topic of our next chapter. You may not identify yourself as a perfectionist, but just wait. You may, like most of us, have some of those tendencies.

4

The Myth of Perfection

Megan, the mother of a fifteen-month-old, lives under the burden of an emotional dictator called perfectionism. She is controlled by lists, achievements, and a spotless home. A beautiful woman with faultless makeup and coordinated wardrobe, Megan wants to be the very best person she can be for her own sake and for her Lord Jesus.

She writes down what she wants to accomplish in a day, but sees the afternoon slip by before she has crossed off all the projects. Frustration begins to build, tension causes her neck muscles to tighten, and when her toddler spills her milk or disobeys, Megan flames into curses at her and wishes she could return to her childless days.

This Christian woman experiences a constant dissatisfaction with what she does and who she is. Always striving to be better, she picks out and concentrates on her slightest error, even when her behavior is acceptable. Megan's three most frequent thoughts about herself are: "I could have done that better," "I should have reacted this way," and "I would have acted differently if only . . ."

Besides feeling dissatisfied with herself, she also has the vague feeling that God is never quite persuaded that she is doing all she can to live for him. When she remembers how

Jesus died for her sins, she condemns herself even more. After all that he has done for her, she should pray more, be a better witness, and apply biblical instruction with greater wisdom. Even if she does "perform" well, Megan can only condemn herself for the small percentage she didn't do right.

It wasn't until Megan began to understand the difference between *perfectionism* and *Christian perfection* that she could accept herself as a person and as a child of God.

Differences between Perfectionism and Christian Perfection

Psychotherapist Karen Horney calls perfectionism "the tyranny of the ought" because of a perfectionist's thinking that he or she ought to have done better. Someone has quipped, "Perfectionists are people who take great pains . . . and pass them on to others."

I know about both those definitions because I constantly used the words "could have," "should have," and "would have," and I definitely took great pains that made myself and others miserable. But over time I learned the difference between perfectionism and Christian perfection. *Perfectionism* is that sense of needing to perform to earn God's acceptance, whereas *Christian perfection* is believing that God already views us as perfect because of our position in Christ. Christian perfection is knowing we are accepted because of the forgiveness we receive when we ask Jesus to be our Lord and Savior. Its truth is expressed in Colossians 2:10: "And in Him you have been made complete." The word *complete* can also be translated "perfect."

David Seamands, in his book *Healing for Damaged Emotions,* says:

There is a great difference between true Christian perfection and perfectionism. Perfectionism is a counterfeit for Christian perfection, holiness, sanctification, or the Spirit-filled life. Instead of making us holy persons and integrated personalities—that is, whole persons in Christ—perfectionism leaves us spiritual Pharisees and emotional neurotics. There is only one ultimate cure for perfectionism: it is as profound and yet as simple as the word grace.[1]

God totally accepts us as Christians, so we no longer need to try to earn salvation or acceptance. In his eyes, we are perfect because we are covered with a mantle of grace and Jesus' righteousness. Unfortunately, we perfectionists are still trying to earn our own mantle of righteousness through our good works.

Never Good Enough

When I was thirteen, I celebrated New Year's Eve by taking a symbolic cleansing bubble bath right at the stroke of midnight. As I lay in the cleansing, warm water after washing my body squeaky clean, I prayed, "God, please forgive everything I've done wrong in my life. I promise I won't do anything else wrong for the rest of my life." Although I attended church at that time, I hadn't yet understood the real purpose in Jesus' death and resurrection. I still pictured God standing up in heaven with his arms crossed in front of his chest, tapping his toe, looking down at me and saying, "Kathy, when are you going to become perfect so that I can truly love you?"

I went to bed that night so pleased with myself, convinced I'd found the way to earn entrance into heaven and a knowledge of God's love. The next morning I just knew I'd begun a new life of perfection. Yet several hours later I discovered my sister, Karen, coloring with my brand-new colored pencils, and I was furious. Screaming my displeasure, I grabbed the pencils out of her hand. In the midst of my anger, the reality of what I was doing hit me. I was getting angry, and I'd vowed only twelve hours before to never do anything wrong again! I couldn't believe I'd failed so quickly. How was I ever going to achieve perfection and earn God's love along with entrance into heaven?

Being the kind of person who doesn't give up easily, I hatched a different plan. *OK, Kathy,* I told myself, *you can't seem to make your life perfect. But certainly you should be able to do more right things than wrong things by the time you die. When God sees what a good girl you are, he'll have to let you into heaven.*

From that point on, my goal became offsetting my bad deeds with good deeds. In my imagination, I kept track of my good deeds on one side of a scale and my bad deeds on the other. As time went along, I was crushed to realize there were always more bad deeds accumulated than good deeds. Of course, I couldn't count something on the good side of the scale unless it was done one hundred percent correctly! Even then my perfectionism was influencing my thinking—without my realizing it.

I really wondered whether I'd qualify for heaven. Would I be able to accumulate more good deeds than bad deeds by the time I died? How was I going to convince God I deserved to enter heaven if I couldn't? How grateful I was when, at the age of eighteen, I heard the gospel message clearly for the first time and recognized God's gift of salvation—a free gift that I could neither earn nor deserve. Once I'd made that decision, I no longer had to keep track of my good and bad deeds. What a glorious freedom!

I thought that freedom would set me completely free from my perfectionist tendencies. Unfortunately it didn't, and ever since, God has been helping me fight my natural tendency to strive for perfection. As a good perfectionist with an all-or-nothing attitude, I think I should be able to perfectly banish perfectionism from my life! But that is indeed a deadly perfectionist attitude. Instead, I must learn to allow the Holy Spirit, rather than the perfectionism, to control me.

But because we perfectionists do not live perfectly—because we are still human—our old nature wars against the Holy Spirit within us. Nevertheless, we need not be discouraged; God is more interested in our progress than in our perfection. He simply wants us to keep growing closer to him.

Even the apostle Paul said late in his life:

Not that I have already obtained it, or have already become perfect, but I press on in order that I may lay hold of that for which also I was laid hold of by Christ Jesus. . . . I do not regard myself as having laid hold of it yet, but one thing I do: forgetting what lies behind and reaching forward to what lies ahead, I press on toward the goal for the prize of the upward call of God in Christ Jesus. (Philippians 3:12-14)

If anyone could reach perfection or full maturity, we would think that Paul could have. Yet he said he had not obtained it. He goes on to say in verse 15, "Let us therefore, as many as are perfect [complete], have this attitude." In verse 12 he says he's not perfect, then he explains in verse 15 that an attitude of perfection is forgetting what lies behind and pressing on toward the call of God.

Perfectionism concentrates on the past and on striving to do what is right through our own efforts. It results in discouragement and self-condemnation because we never can measure up in our own power. *Christian perfection is forgiving our mistakes and focusing on becoming more like Jesus by relaxing in the Holy Spirit's power to control us.*

The Causes of Perfectionism

Perfectionism can have several causes. Perhaps our parents offered us only *conditional love.* Even though we're adults now, we may believe we won't receive our parents' acceptance unless we perform according to their expectations for perfection.

Perfectionism can also result from our varying *temperaments.* People with a melancholy temperament tend to be very hard on themselves when they don't perform at their own high standards. My own struggle against perfectionism stems from that very cause—my melancholy, analytical temperament. My parents were loving, supportive, and accepting, yet somehow I never measured up to who I thought I should be and what I thought I should do. I didn't recognize my perfectionism until many years ago, when I tried to raise strong-willed Darcy. She unknowingly helped me see my attitudes for what they really were: unrealistic and perfectionistic.

Therein lies one of perfectionism's problems: We don't always recognize it at first. After all, I did not have unrealistic standards for everything I did, so I didn't classify myself as a perfectionist. I was content to sew an imperfect dress; I could handle preparing a meal that wasn't gourmet; I often allowed a room to stay messy; and if I was hurried enough, I could go out of the house without putting on makeup.

But the standard that was most important to me—what other people thought of me—I could not lower. When my daughter didn't behave angelically in public, I became furious later on. If anyone saw that messy room or noticed the flaw in my dress, I felt unacceptable. It was all right for *me* to know of my imperfections, but not for anyone else to notice. At the foundation of wanting to be perfect was my knowledge of how inadequate I really was. I constantly tried to say to myself and especially to others, "Look! I am worth something. See how perfectly I do everything?" But inside I still felt inadequate, because I saw myself as a failure in so many areas. So I tried all the more to be perfect and hide the truth.

My high expectations and feelings of inadequacy boiled to the surface when Darcy demanded more love from me than I thought I possessed. How much love could I give her when I didn't even love myself? It was frustrating. Then, in my efforts to preserve whatever bit of self-esteem I had, I pushed her away. I didn't want her to expose my inadequacy.

This is how perfectionism is connected to self-image. *It is merely compensation for inadequacy and a cover-up for poor self-esteem.* Anger results because we feel threatened. We strive to become what is impossible without the Holy Spirit's power.

Unfortunately, our perfectionism intensely affects our parenting role and abilities. Looking back now, I can see that the unrealistic expectations stemming from my perfectionism took away much of the joy of raising two children.

When Darcy was in elementary school and began expressing her own personality in her clothes, I felt frustrated because her tastes were so different from mine. In my narrow, perfectionist thinking, I felt she should prefer the same things I did. When she wanted to dress casually in pants and a top for church, I felt threatened. I love to wear dresses and believed church required more dressing up. At first I thought Darcy's choice of clothing for church meant she was rebelling against

God. I overreacted, forcing her to wear dresses, which only created a power struggle between us.

Eventually I understood that Darcy feels more comfortable in casual clothing and has a more dramatic personality. I, on the other hand, love elegance and formal attire. I am more subdued in my behavior. That wasn't Darcy at all. When I finally realized that her opinions stemmed from mere clothing preferences, and not rebellion, I could begin to let her be herself. She no longer had to perform according to my definition of what was "perfect" for church. The important thing was that she wanted to go to church.

Another way my perfectionism surfaced was my need for Darcy and Mark to react perfectly. If they didn't, I blamed myself for their disobedience. In fact, everything seemed like it was my fault. We perfectionists are great at taking the blame for everything.

Passing the Burden of Perfectionism On

Not only does this mind-set affect our reactions, it can also influence our children to develop their own perfectionist perspective. Although that may not be our intention, it can happen when we react in these ways.

1. If we are never satisfied with what they've done, we can give our children the impression they must be perfect to please us. I remember visiting with a friend when her daughter came home from kindergarten. The little girl ran up to her mommy and happily showed her the papers she had colored at school. My friend's first words were, "Look how you colored outside the lines." The little girl's face fell in disappointment, but her mother didn't seem to notice. I knew my friend had been a school teacher before having her children, and I concluded that her teaching instincts were surfacing. Unfortunately, I think they made the little girl believe she couldn't please her mother.

Of course we want to correct our children and help them to do better. But if our instruction isn't accompanied by primarily encouraging, positive comments, we may be actually teaching them to disobey. When we give more negative comments than positive comments, the child may get the impression that the only way to get our attention is to disobey. How much better to "catch them being good," as someone has said.

I often suggest in my parenting seminars that mothers and fathers put on a tape recorder when they know they're going to have some time interacting with their children. Later they can listen to the tape and keep track of how many positive and negative comments they give their child. If there are more negative ones than positive, that child may be disobeying because it's the only way to get much needed attention.

2. We can develop perfectionism in our children when we compare them with others. Sometimes we think such comparisons are a good way of motivating them to good behavior, but usually the child doesn't see it that way. I remember interviewing a woman who struggled in her adult years with bulimia. God delivered her, but during her healing process she recognized how inferior she had felt in her father's eyes. She remembers bringing her report card home and after her dad would look it over, he would ask her, "How did your friend Susie do on her report card?"

She was crushed. She felt as though she never measured up. Many years later her healing process brought the light of understanding on that situation. Her father explained that he hadn't intended to compare her with her friend, only that he knew of Susie's troubled home life and was concerned about Susie's academic progress.

How easy it is for our children to misinterpret our intentions. That means we must guard our tongue even more carefully.

3. We may develop perfectionism in our children by not giving them admiration and physical attention. Although it's hard to believe anyone could still believe that praising children will cause them to develop a "big head," at times we may praise only those things which are important to us. That could come across to a child as lack of admiration.

My son Mark, now nineteen years old, has played the drums since junior high. Over the years he gained bigger and louder drum sets—and believe me, the neighborhood knows when Mark is practicing. When I tell other people that Mark is a drummer, I often see people wrinkle their nose and exclaim, "Ugh, you must really hate that." I can imagine them not being able to praise their children if they chose such a noisy instrument. But I think Mark's interest is great. I loved watching him in the junior high and high school bands, and I don't mind him practicing at all. I do have to shut some doors at times to talk on the phone, but knowing Mark has such a healthy interest is wonderful. It's easy for me to praise and admire him for his skills, even though others might not appreciate such an accomplishment.

In Ross Campbell's books *How to Really Love Your Child* and *How to Really Love Your Teenager,* he stresses the importance of showing physical affection to our children. He says it helps to fill up their "emotional tank." I think it also helps them know we love and accept them unconditionally, and that's a preventive device against perfectionist tendencies.

Willard F. Harley, Jr., in his book *His Needs/Her Needs,* says that when a husband gives affection to his wife, he is giving her three messages: "You are important to me; I'll take care of you," "I'm concerned about things that matter to you," and "I'm proud of you and what you're doing." I think those three messages are communicated to our children as well when we give them affection.

4. We may communicate a perfectionistic attitude if we try to fulfill our lost dreams through our child. Parents can give their kids the message, "Do what I want you to do, not what you're destined to do." Josh Billings said, "To bring up a child in the way he should go, travel that way yourself once in a while." It's the parent who wants to force a child down a predetermined path who gives that child the feeling that he or she is acceptable only as an extension of the parent, not simply as himself or herself. I'm sure you meet people, like I do, who are still trying to gain the approval and applause of their parents. If they never receive that approval, they will always be trying to be perfect so that maybe then their mother or father will accept them.

By seeing our children through God's eyes and by being open to however God wants to use them or lead them, we'll make them feel as if they don't have to perform according to our expectations or fulfill the dreams we were unable to live out in our own lives.

Striving versus Relaxing

In order to combat these tendencies that will pass perfectionism along to our children, we need to relax in the Holy Spirit's power, instead of striving to become perfect. We can tell that we are striving in our own power when we are tense, angry, or condemning ourselves. It's like an emotional "gritting of our teeth." When I'm seeing the opposite of the fruit of the Spirit in my life—critical thinking instead of love, discontentment instead of joy, anxiety instead of peace, anger instead of patience, disregard for the feelings of others instead of kindness, sinful actions instead of goodness, insensitivity instead of gentleness, irresponsibility instead of faithfulness, and out-of-control reactions instead of self-control—I know I'm striving in my own power.

Now when I begin to feel that kind of tension and effort, I stop, close my eyes, take several deep breaths, and imagine the Holy Spirit flowing into me. I focus on who I am in Christ and the power I have as a Christian. As a result, I usually feel a release of that tension and sense an inner power to react and behave the way the Lord wants me to. I have renewed peace and confidence that God will work in me.

As I rely on God, I sometimes need to give up some expectations that I'd determined were so important, or forgive someone, or remind myself that if I'm late the world won't cave in. I also may need to review the admonition to "cease striving and know that I am God" (Psalm 46:10). I have found tremendous victory in diminishing perfectionism as I've concentrated on who God truly is. Focusing on his graciousness, mercy, faithfulness, forgiveness, and many other attributes wipes out the wrong ideas I carried about him before (like the idea that he was impatiently waiting for me to become perfect). Then as I meditate on his great love for me, I'm reassured all the more. As someone said, "There's nothing you can do to make God love you more, and there's nothing you can do to make him love you less."

God doesn't want us to try harder; he wants us to relax and believe that he will perform through us. We still have to make choices, but when we focus on the Lord and give him permission to take over our reactions and desires, he enables us to choose righteously.

Notice Your Emotional Reactions

You can tell whether you are striving or relaxing by noticing your emotional reactions. If you are striving, you will experience tension, anger, irritation, or other unpleasant feelings. But if you are relaxing in God's control, you'll sense peace, love, self-control, and the other fruit of the Spirit listed in Galatians 5:22-23.

When I sing in a choir, I'm very aware of the value of relaxing. I'm not a very good vocalist, but when I sing alongside a strong alto, my voice becomes strong and stays on key. I feel relaxed, knowing I have her support. That's how it is when we cooperate with the Spirit. We relax in his control by believing that he's going to work in and through us.

Paul demonstrated that belief when he wrote, "For I am confident of this very thing, that He who began a good work in you will perfect it until the day of Christ Jesus" (Philippians 1:6).

When I share that verse in my presentations about gaining godly self-esteem, I will often quote it this way: "For I am confident of this very thing, that He who began a good work in you will perfect it *yesterday*." Usually it takes several seconds for those in the audience to catch on. Then I hear giggles throughout the auditorium, reflecting their knowledge that that's the way we really want it to happen. We don't want to have to struggle in life with trials and problems; we want to be instantly perfect, like "how about yesterday?"

Such a perspective, though, creates anger. When we're striving for perfection, impatience with people and especially our children mars our good intentions to be loving parents. We need to again focus on the fact that God has confidence in our process of growth—not process of perfection—for he is the one maturing us. He knows he isn't finished with us yet! He's not in a hurry, either, because he already views us as a finished product.

Mary, a parent who struggles in this area, is beginning to feel assured that God is changing her. She wrote me, saying:

> I always thought the Lord was providing all my strength, but it's amazing to discover what areas of our lives we hold onto and operate by our own power, rather than by God's. I was touched by that because I realized that I didn't concede to God every part of my life, because of either ignorance or the idea that "I can handle this area myself; it's too silly an area to bother God with."
>
> So I prayed that God would help me recognize my need for his guidance in *all* things. I believe that's what he was (and is) doing. It *has* been hard, but now the fruit is beginning to show, and I'm starting to enjoy the kids more and look forward to my time with them. I still have my moments, . . . but God is helping me put out the fires of anger much more quickly.

As you and I continue in our process of growth to diminish perfectionism, we're going to be able to echo Mary's report. We won't ever become perfect, but we will become pleased with our progress.

The next area we'll concentrate on is unrealistic expectations. Most of us have a hard time deciding what is reasonable to expect from ourselves and our children. Let's examine how our expectations relate to our frustration.

5

Great Expectations

Elizabeth and her two-year-old daughter, Carrie, were visiting with Judy and her three-year-old son, Erik. Elizabeth and Judy talked as the children played on the floor. Carrie continually yanked Erik's toys away and he began to cry.

"Carrie, you need to share with Erik," Elizabeth coaxed. But again and again the little girl kept taking the toys away, as Elizabeth became more and more embarrassed. *I bet Judy thinks I'm a terrible mother,* thought Elizabeth. *I want Carrie to share, but I just don't know how to get her to do it.* She continued to try to help her daughter play cooperatively, but nothing worked.

As she worried about Judy's possible critical thoughts, she became more and more upset with herself. Finally, in a burst of exasperation, Elizabeth grabbed Carrie by the arm, slapped her bottom hard, and reprimanded her, "You start sharing right now or we're going home." Looking away from Judy's startled glance, she blushed in embarrassment and tried to distract her crying daughter with a toy.

Does any of this sound familiar? This scene is an example of *displacement—the transference of an emotion to an object which is logically inappropriate.* Note how Elizabeth transferred her own embarrassment into anger at her daughter. And much of her embarrassment came from unrealistic expectations of herself and of her daughter.

Dealing With Displacement

As I look back to those angry times in my life, I can see how I often expected too much, and also displaced my feelings. Often I was irritated or angry with Larry or myself, but because I couldn't manage that situation, I leveled my frustration against an innocent bystander, Darcy. She usually had not done anything bad enough to deserve my blow-up; she was just the nearest object that couldn't strike back. I usually blamed Darcy for my outbursts, thinking her disobedience caused my anger. Now I know her behavior was only the straw that broke the back of my patience. Other situations and relationships were at play, but I didn't see their influence or significance.

If we can begin to see when we displace our anger from the real cause to our children, we'll be on our way to learning godly reactions to their disobedience. The best way to prevent displacement is to *deal with each situation or problem as it occurs, instead of storing them up*. By recognizing potential situations for displacing our anger, we can stop ourselves from spilling out other problems onto our children's misbehavior.

Now let's go back to Elizabeth and revise that scene. As Elizabeth and Judy talk, the children play on the floor. Carrie continually yanks Erik's toys away, making him cry. Disconcerted with her daughter's behavior, Elizabeth comments to Judy, "I feel so embarrassed when Carrie doesn't share. I just don't know what to do about it."

"Oh, don't worry about it," Judy responds. "It's perfectly normal for a two-year-old not to share. My son has learned to share only in the last couple of weeks."

"Oh, really? Well, I guess she'll learn someday, too!" Elizabeth breathes a sigh of relief and settles into the sofa to enjoy the visit.

Of course, not every situation will turn out well just because we share our feelings. But by recognizing those feelings and trying to deal with them, we can prevent displacement. Even if we cannot change our situation, we still will release the pressure that is building inside of us. Dr. Theodore Rubin puts it this way: "Big blow-ups are really accumulated results of repressed, potential, small, air-cleaning blow-ups."

Denise shared with me that one evening she felt angry about having to do the dishes while her two young sons and husband relaxed watching television. Instead of continuing to dwell on it, she stood near them and screamed at the top of her voice. After they jumped in fright, and she explained why she yelled, they continued to watch television, and she finished the dishes—laughing and happy. She says that if she hadn't done that right then, she most likely would have stewed about it all night and taken out her pent-up anger on her little boys the next day.

I'm not advising you to scream and scare everyone. Instead, ask your family to help you with the dishes! But I do hope you'll communicate and declare your feelings as soon as they occur.

A second tool for preventing displacement is to *find the real reason for your anger.* Ask yourself, "Am I really angry at this present situation, or is something else bothering me?" Most of the time, your child's present disobedience is not the main thing you're angry about. By finding the real cause of your anger and dealing with that, you won't displace it onto someone else.

Our Child, a Reflection?

Another common cause for anger is the expectation that our child should behave because he or she is a reflection of who we are. Elizabeth, in our earlier example, believed her daughter's lack of sharing meant she was a terrible parent. *When we can separate our own sense of worth from the behavior of our children,* we're on our way to dealing with anger more effectively.

Unfortunately, most parents have difficulty doing that, as I did. In an effort to help them process this new information, I often ask them, "Your child is having a temper tantrum on the grocery store floor; how do you feel?" Mothers, in particular, report they feel embarrassed, annoyed, angry, frustrated, tense, and myriad other unpleasant feelings.

I go on to point out that those feelings indicate we are thinking our child is a reflection of us. That belief often is bolstered by an older woman who walks by, looks down at the screaming child, then looks up at us—and we know what she's thinking: *Bad child . . . bad mother.* Society believes that it is possible to always control a child, even a child determined to scream bloody murder!

Betty Coble Lawther, author of the book *Woman Aware and Choosing,* says we are responsible to train our child, but we are not responsible for the decisions our child makes. This truth can set us free. Our anger feeds on believing the lie that we can always control our child. The truth is we cannot. We can do our best and even consistently give discipline and training, but our child can still choose to disobey. Even if it were somehow possible for us to be a perfect parent (oh, don't I wish!), our child would still act like a child—because he or she *is* a child.

I have the perfect retort for that woman who gives us that condemning look (you may want to take two steps back first in case she's a violent person): "The umbilical cord was cut when he was born." That theme is reinforced as we consider that we all know good parents who have rebellious children, and we know poor parents who have good kids. Beyond our parenting skills, many things affect the choices our children make: their own temperament, their school experiences, the way they view life. Yet if we take responsibility for everything our children do, we're saying we can monitor, control, and manage every minute of their lives.

Every Child Is Different

I know this concept is difficult for many to believe. At one seminar where I discussed these ideas, a woman raised her hand and said, "I really disagree with your ideas. I know my child is a good child because I'm a good mother." I couldn't help but notice the light laughter in the room.

I asked, "How many children do you have?" "One," she replied. I respectfully added, "Please be sure to have another." Although it came across as funny and everyone laughed, it states the truth. So often a second child who is strong-willed and unlike a compliant first child, will show us that our parenting skills are only one of many influences upon that new little person. Their temperament, personality, and degree of compliance or strong will also forcefully influence the decisions they make.

I didn't understand this when Darcy was little. I hadn't even heard the term *strong-willed child.* I just interpreted everything

Darcy did wrong as meaning she didn't like me. Once I identified her as being strong-willed, I no longer had to take her behavior personally or condemn myself for being such a horrible mother. What freedom to accept Darcy for what she was and still is—an assertive person who helps me to say no to the salesman at the door and who has no trouble asking for what she wants.

I've talked with so many parents who can't believe the differences between their children. They are the same parents, reacting the same way to both children, in the same home environment, yet the two children can be totally opposite. If the theory were true that our children are a reflection of us, we could count on them being the same.

When I think of this concept, I'm often reminded of God's reaction to Adam and Eve in the Garden of Eden after they had sinned. Suppose God, as their heavenly Father, had begun to wring his hands and lament, "Oh, I'm just so bothered about Adam and Eve sinning. I guess I'm just not a very good parent to them. If I'd really done a good job, they wouldn't have chosen to sin." How ridiculous. God didn't take responsibility for his "children's" disobedience. Instead he lovingly confronted them (see Genesis 3).

Neither did Jesus feel bad about himself when his disciples didn't measure up after all the training he had given them. Deuteronomy 24:16 says, "Fathers shall not be put to death for their sons, nor shall sons be put to death for their fathers; everyone shall be put to death for his own sin." We are ultimately responsible only for our own behavior and choices.

As parents, we need to do the very best we can in raising our children. That may mean taking parenting classes, reading books, and getting advice from other people. As time goes along, we will progress in our parenting skills. We'll never become perfect, but we can remind ourselves we're doing the best we can and then trust God for the future.

Understanding Child Development

As we have said, when we feel angry toward our children, it is generally good to first do a self-check to try and determine the true source of that anger. Sometimes we may find that we are displacing. But there are times when that is not true, and our children are the direct cause of our anger. Let's look into some of those situations.

One of the main reasons our children make us angry is *because we have unrealistic expectations of their behavior.* We believe they can do or understand something, when in reality they can't. Then when they disobey or misbehave, we get angry.

That's what happened to a young mother I recently observed in a department store. Her six- or seven-year-old daughter had begged to push the stroller that held her one-year-old brother. The mother finally relented, and as the little girl followed her mother, trying to maneuver the lightweight stroller between the racks of clothes, the stroller tipped over. Her mother turned and saw her daughter straining with all her might to stand it back up again. The woman immediately righted the stroller and, with a fierce scowl, yelled at the little girl, "Now look what you've done." She instantly smacked her daughter's bottom. Tears sprang into the little girl's eyes, and she hung her head in fear and humiliation.

Similar incidents happen many times a day across America. The situations are different, but the underlying cause is the same: an overstressed parent expects too much from a child. When the child fails or doesn't meet the parent's expectations, the parent becomes angry and overreacts.

Please don't think I'm condemning the mother in this example. I've been in her shoes. She most likely had a to-do list a mile long, wanted to get a gift quickly in the store, and had listened all day to her daughter's constant chatter. When the stroller tipped over, it was just too much. She had reached her frustration level, and she believed that her daughter had pushed the stroller over on purpose.

In situations like this, we expect children to do something that they are not ready to handle. They are not there yet in their emotional or physical development. That mother in the store wasn't wrong to allow her daughter to push the stroller, but when it tipped over, she could have thought, *Well, that stroller is a lot for her to handle. My getting upset is not going to make her stronger or go back in time to prevent the accident.* Looking at our child's abilities more realistically can help diffuse the tension.

I've often felt uptight because someone else's child could do something that Darcy couldn't—at the same age. But it creates unnecessary problems when we compare children with other children. When I take into account the individual differences, personalities, and temperaments of each unique child, it helps balance my perspective.

Child development is a prime area where parents lack training. Most of the time we don't know what to expect or we are uninformed about the developmental patterns of our children. We expect too much, are disappointed, and react in anger and frustration. Instead, parents can take advantage of the many books available that outline the approximate ages at which children can do things. If you can't afford to buy one, the library has many. The government also offers pamphlets on child development. But don't forget that every child has his or her own developmental schedule and may not exactly follow the "textbook" cases.

If you think you might be expecting too much from your child and are getting angry as a result, refer to a child development book. Make a list of the things you can expect from your child at his age. Affix the list to your refrigerator. Then, when your child does something that is listed, before dealing with the child, walk to the refrigerator, make a check mark by that action, and realize that your child is only doing what is normal for his or her age level.

Does he spill his milk at every meal? Check it off. Does she scribble on the walls? Check it off. Does he mess up his room with toys and have difficulty putting them away? Check it off. After you've checked the behavior and realize that it can be expected, you can go back to the child and discipline him calmly and effectively.

Many times children displease their parent because they are going through a developmental phase. Maybe they say "no" to everything, or stutter, or want to do everything themselves. Once you understand that the child will grow out of it, you can relax. Quite often, the sooner the parent accepts it, the sooner unwanted behavior goes away.

Additional Unrealistic Expectations

When Darcy was a baby, I once stood in line to get her picture taken. I was chatting with two sisters, both of whom had toddlers around two years old. We were talking about the different phases children go through, and one sister commented that her daughter was going through a "cussing phase." Her sister looked astonished at her and observed, "She wouldn't cuss if you didn't."

How true! *Often our actions influence our children's behavior, and then we get angry at them for acting that way!* We might become angry because our child is mirroring a bad habit of ours—and we don't want to be reminded that we have it. For example, Darcy's whining often aggravates me, and then I remember that I often complain to God about my circumstances.

God uses children to mature us, and when they start acting like we do, we feel put down a notch. Sometimes, we don't even realize why we're so upset with them, but it's because they're doing what God has been telling us not to do.

Another cause of anger is that *we expect our children to be well-behaved when they're too tired to be.* I've often regretted trying to fit my children into my schedule. At times I've continued shopping, knowing my children were getting too tired or too hungry to go on. Then my communication became battle cries of, "Stop whining," "We'll be home for lunch in a few minutes," "Stop poking your brother," and "Get off the floor!" Whatever few, harried minutes of shopping I gained by continuing with my plans, I paid for with irritation and anger.

I also realized I was expecting my children to be able to ignore all the things they shouldn't touch in our home when their curiosity overrided their self-control. As a result, I gave in and child-proofed my home. They have enough temptations to teach them self-control that cannot be "put away," without leaving out forbidden objects that could be removed. Why tempt our own power to control *ourselves* when our little one breaks the family heirlooms that we wanted out? In the future, we will have plenty of time to display our favorite knickknacks.

Children need a safe place to play where they can have fun and expend their energy without fear of discipline for knocking over furniture. If you live in an apartment and don't have a yard, make a point to go to a park or even walk a couple of blocks so that your child can vent his God-given energy. Being cooped up isn't good for him—or you!

I love to tell the story about the father and his toddler daughter who were walking through a national forest. The father instructed his daughter, "Stay on the path, honey." But she continually ran back and forth, hither and yon, noticing every tree, bird, and flower. Several times he told her to stay on the path, and each time he became increasingly irritated. Finally, he grabbed her arm and said through gritted teeth, "I said stay on the path." She looked up at him in wide-eyed amazement and asked, "What's a path, Daddy?"

Our expectations of our children must take into account that *they don't have the same knowledge we do.* Sometimes they don't know what a path is, or how to make the bed, or what is involved in cleaning the bathroom.

Consider for a moment what it must be like to be a child. You have adults telling you what to do, but you don't understand what a word means or how to do what they want. They must feel as helpless as I would have if, before I was computer literate, a computer expert had set a personal computer in front of me and said, "Load this disk into the computer's memory."

Having never seen a computer before, I would probably ask, "How do you do it?"

"Well, it's very simple. I can do it in seconds," he replies. "Just do it."

In the computer expert's brain, a procedure as simple as loading a disk is a one-step process. But for me, it's a multi-faceted procedure because I don't know where to start. And sometimes your child doesn't know where to start either. You may tell her to make the bed, something you've done for many years. Obviously, it's a simple task. But not for her. Therefore you have to break it down into steps: "First you take off the pillow. Then pull back the sheet and blanket. Now smooth the bottom sheet, etc." If we could look at our interaction with our children through their eyes, we quickly would see when our expectations are too high and become overwhelming for them.

A mother gazed down at her screaming and kicking child laying on the grocery store floor. She angrily muttered to an older woman passing by, "Look at him. It's disgusting. He's acting just like a two-year-old!"

The woman whispered, "How old is he?"

The mother looked amazed at first. Then her face relaxed into a smile as she replied in embarrassment, "Oh, he *is* two years old. I guess he's acting his age, isn't he?" Let's be realistic in what we want and expect from our child.

High Expectations of Ourselves

Another way we can have unrealistic expectations that can cause anger is believing *we can meet all our child's needs.* How frustrated we can become when we try and fail to do that, as we surely will, because it's impossible to totally meet anyone's needs. In fact, in many instances, God wants our children to fail. When we rescue them, we have protected them from God's discipline and process of growth.

Proverbs 19:19 is usually applied to adults, but I think it can also apply to our children: "A man [child] of great anger shall bear the penalty, for if you rescue him, you will only have to do it again." And again . . . and again. That principle applies to more than just an angry person; it applies to the child who forgets to take his lunch to school and the mother discovers it and takes it over to him. Then she wonders why he's so forgetful. It's because he's never suffered for his forgetfulness. If she were to let him be hungry—it might take only one time—he'd most likely remember his lunch.

Here are some situations you might want to avoid as possible "rescue operations" with your children:

- Giving a consequence for their misbehavior and then not following through
- Doing their homework for them
- Making excuses for their disobedient behavior before others
- Taking forgotten homework to school for them
- Bringing in their bike at night without giving them a consequence

I've struggled with these issues myself. When Mark was thirteen years old, he wanted to go to a Christian golf camp in Florida. We live in California. We were thrilled that he wanted to go and bought a plane ticket that required him to change planes in Dallas. As he packed that day, I tried to instruct him on how to find his gate on the monitor in Dallas for the connecting flight. I knew from being there that the Dallas airport is huge and travelers often have to go to a different terminal to find their next flight. As usual, he interpreted my helpfulness as meaning he was incompetent. But I knew he had never referred to a monitor before and so I tried to persist. He still shunned my instruction.

After seeing him off at the airport, I felt anxious. I just knew he was going to miss his flight in Dallas. For the next three hours, I nervously puttered around the house, and when I knew it was time for him to change planes in Dallas, I stayed close to the phone, convinced he would be calling to ask for my advice.

Suddenly, I sensed the Lord gently whisper in my heart, "You want him to fail, don't you? Let him need me." I was shocked! Want him to fail? Of course I didn't want him to fail.

When God repeated his gentle accusation, I had to consider it seriously. *Lord, I just know he doesn't understand how to find his way. But I guess I honestly do want to be involved in his life. Yes, I guess I want to be needed. You're right. Please forgive me. Let him need you, but please keep Mark safe!*

Several hours later the phone rang. It was Mark! He was in Florida, safe and sound. "How did you find your flight in Dallas?" I eagerly asked him.

"Oh, Mom," his voice scolded. "I just wandered up and down the aisle until I found it."

Wandered up and down the aisle until he found it? My heart skipped a beat. Yet at the same time I felt strangely confident. Wasn't that just like God to take care of him?

That day I took a step closer to releasing Mark and giving up the unrealistic expectation that I could meet all his needs. Only by knowing God would hold him in his everlasting arms could I continue that process. I have told many parents that *our children need to be needy so that they will need God.* Even if we could meet all their needs, we wouldn't really want to, because then they would not be challenged to depend upon God.

Our Children's Temperaments

Julie and I were talking over lunch one day when she mentioned, "Aaron made me so angry the other day. That kid will do something wrong and glibly say he's sorry. Before I know it, he's done the same thing again and repeats his quick 'I'm sorry,' as if it makes everything better. I just don't understand how he can experience such a lack of remorse."

I knew her son Aaron. As a twelve-year-old, he was a kick to have around. Always smiling, never angry, he was the life of the party and made everyone he met feel like a long lost friend. I commiserated with Julie's frustration, but said,

"Y'know, Aaron's attitude about being sorry is completely in line with his temperament."

Julie looked at me in surprise. "What do you mean?" I went on to discuss the four temperaments and how knowing about them has helped me to be more patient with my children, understanding and aware of God's possible purposes for their life.

Although many people use the terms *melancholy, sanguine, choleric,* and *phlegmatic* to describe the temperaments, my husband Larry and I teach this concept with different terms, which we find more user-friendly. We say a person is either an *Analytical,* an *Expressive,* a *Driver,* or an *Amiable.* Here's a brief description of each one.

- *Analytical:* This person's main goal in life is to make life perfect. Analyticals are organized, detail-oriented, idealistic, and creative in writing and art. They tend to be more interested in accomplishments than relating to people. They love to research before making decisions, but as a result can often be struck with "analysis paralysis." (This is my temperament, so I know it's the perfect temperament!)

- *Expressive:* This person's main goal in life is to have fun! Expressives are the life of every party. They are very people-oriented and as a result are not interested in details, organization, or getting much accomplished. They can make quick decisions, usually based on emotion. They are filled with enthusiasm, ideas, and big dreams.

- *Driver:* This person's main goal in life is to be in control. Drivers are natural leaders and shine when they are in charge. They make quick decisions and base them on

fact and logic. Since they are action-oriented, they can
easily step on other people's toes, especially since they usually are confident they are right. (This is Larry's temperament, and he assures me *it's* the perfect temperament!)

- *Amiable:* This person's main goal in life is to have peace
  at any cost. Amiables are people-oriented like expressives, but they would rather be in the background than
  up front. They are great negotiators and make great world
  ambassadors because they can mediate between warring
  factions. They judge the value of becoming involved in
  activity based upon how much energy is required—since
  they don't usually feel very energetic.

As you can see, *every temperament has strengths and weaknesses.* There is no perfect temperament. When we understand
these temperaments, though, we can better understand and accept
ourselves and the people around us—especially our children.
If we don't apply the knowledge about the temperaments, we
can easily become exasperated with our children because their
perspective on life may be different than ours.

For instance, as an analytical, I can easily clash with my
daughter, who is a driver. When she was little, I felt insecure
in my mothering role, and Darcy was very willing to take
charge of the household. I can remember Darcy turning thirteen and telling me, "Mom, I'm a teenager now. I ought to
be able to make all my own decisions." At other times, she
commented on my disciplining of Mark, telling me what I
really should have done. At first these comments bothered me.
But as I reviewed my commitment to not take things personally, and realized she is a driver, I knew I needed to be strong
and consistent in my mothering skills so that I could be the
parent. Knowing about the temperaments helped me to relate
to her in an appropriate way.

You can certainly begin to see the possible difficulties if, say, a mother is a driver and her son is an amiable. Unless she understood the temperaments, she would constantly be frustrated with her son who didn't have strong opinions, when she felt strongly about everything! Since she makes quick decisions but her child doesn't, she could come across as harsh and unloving as she constantly exhorts him, "Just make a decision!"

Another potential toxic combination is an expressive parent and analytical child. The parent would always be wanting to have fun and not be very consistent in discipline. The child might feel slighted as his need for order and organization goes unmet. He may inwardly crave the security of a scheduled life (though most children won't admit it), yet this expressive parent rarely keeps to a schedule.

I've heard from some expressive moms who say that all the neighborhood kids love to come to her house to play because she's involved with the kids and is always creating fun. Unfortunately, she reports that her child may actually grow tired of sharing Mom with everyone.

Earlier I shared Julie's frustration with her expressive son, Aaron. Julie is an analytical and was hurt that Aaron didn't show great remorse and try harder to never "sin" again. That is what an analytical would want in her efforts to become perfect. But an expressive flits from one idea to the next and hardly has time to dwell upon something, like remorse, that isn't fun.

You can begin to see that understanding the temperaments can release a lot of unrealistic expectations. Such an understanding doesn't negate the need for us to train our children in ways that might be the opposite of their natural tendencies. Our goal should be to develop versatility within them, and teach the concept *that each of us can choose to operate in the strengths of another temperament through the power of the Holy Spirit.* Although we can be sensitive to the inner workings of our children and how our personality relates to theirs, we'll still need to encourage them to make right choices. The temperaments aren't a cop-out for poor behavior, but a knowledge of them can diminish our anger.

So far we've reviewed several "great expectations" that can create anger. If you want to work on reshaping your expectations, try writing the following reminders on a card:

- Am I displacing an emotion inappropriately?
- My child isn't a reflection of me.
- My child can be expected to act like a child.
- Maybe it's a "temperament" thing.

Post this card on your refrigerator or mirror as a reminder of some of the ideas we've covered in this chapter. Then read on to find some practical solutions to defusing your anger, when counting to 10 just isn't enough.

6

If Only My Spouse Would Change . . .

For several months Sarah had been sharing with me her struggle with anger. Whenever I related how God had healed my relationship with Larry, Sarah always insisted that there was no disunity between her and her husband. She believed her problems were never caused by her husband's inadequacies—because he had said they weren't! When I said I thought he had some weaknesses, she seemed surprised. It was very difficult at first for her to realize that his reactions contributed to her anger problem. As time passed, though, she began to become more aware of how their disagreements and problems were affecting her parental reactions.

When my temper was out of control, I was not like Sarah. I was only too eager to see my husband's flaws. The more I dwelled on his failings, the more dissatisfied and unhappy I became, with him and with life. It wasn't until I began to feel better about myself that I stopped trying to change Larry. Then God changed him.

Decide to Love

I'll never forget how God propelled that change into happening. I had begun to identify some of the causes of my anger toward Darcy and was reacting toward her with more patience and love. I was thrilled! I could really see God working, and I had hope for the first time. Yet there was still one major source of anger and discontentment: my relationship with Larry. He still was working two jobs and flew an airplane for a hobby. He rarely took us along with him. On one particular day, he had gone flying again, and I was furious!

Later in the afternoon, I was picking up around the house, when I suddenly sensed God whisper in my heart, "I want you to tell Larry you love him." I couldn't believe it. That was the farthest thing from the truth. *I will not, Lord. It's not true, and I won't be a hypocrite! You know I hate his guts and his plane can crash for all I care.*

Then the Lord whispered again, "I want you to tell Larry you love him." I couldn't believe God was being so persistent. How could he ask such a thing? If I told Larry that, he would think I was approving of everything he was doing wrong. And knowing him, he'd think of something else to keep him away from the house even more often—as if that were possible! *No, I won't say it, Lord. He'll just use it against me.*

By the third time God whispered, he'd changed the message a little: "Then, Kathy, I want you to *think* it the next time you see Larry." Think it? What possible good would that do? He wouldn't even hear me. Then I considered it for a moment or two and saw it in a different light. If I thought it, then he couldn't use it against me. *Well, of course then, I'll be your obedient servant, Lord.*

All that day I geared myself up to think those three little words, *I love you,* that I hadn't said or felt for more than two years. That evening, Larry arrived home and walked down the hallway toward me. I told myself, *I'm going to do it. I'm going to say it.* I looked him right in the eye, took a deep breath, gulped, and then thought, *I love you.* Seconds later, I added, *But I don't really.*

I could not comprehend that those three words were true. As far as I was concerned, my love for Larry was dead and nothing could bring it back to life. But the most amazing thing happened! I found my love for him being resurrected. Once I'd made the decision to love Larry, even though the feelings weren't there, and as I continued to make that decision to love him, my feelings began to return. I remembered why I'd been so attracted to him in the first place. The more I focused on the positives, the more loving I felt and the less anger I showed.

Let God Change People

From that experience I learned that choosing to love Larry didn't mean I was approving of his behavior. I could love him yet still disagree with his behavior. I'd always thought loving meant approving. Now, as I chose love, I wasn't as angry about his inadequacies as a husband. I could calmly discuss my expectations.

But more important, *I began to give up my unrealistic expectations that Larry was responsible for my happiness and contentment.* All this time, I had been waiting for Larry to change and meet my needs so that I could be happy and content. God finally got through my wrong thinking and let me know that only he could meet my needs. Larry was just as needy as I was, yet I thought he should be my all in all.

What a difference it made once I released Larry from such a burden! When I wasn't so angry, he started to want to spend more time with me. Eventually he agreed to go with me on a couples' retreat, where God began the healing process within us. I found out that Larry really did love me; he was just showing it in a way *I* didn't interpret as love—by providing for his family.

Two months after that initial retreat, Larry finalized his plans of quitting his job at one police department and being hired by another. But it required a cut in pay, which meant he didn't have as much money to fly! I couldn't believe it. God had created changes in his own timing and in his own method; changes I'd tried to create with years of nagging, control, and manipulation. My faith grew as I saw God's faithfulness to meet my needs in his way.

As time went along, I had to continue to accept the fact that I wasn't perfect and neither was Larry. Just as I was dissatisfied with some of his characteristics and actions, so he was unhappy with elements of my life. We had to accept each other at our levels of maturity. Every relationship is imperfect, because everybody has flaws. But, praise the Lord, God isn't finished with us yet!

God can do a much better job of changing our spouse than we can. He runs a very successful business changing lives, and he's very good at it. He knows our mate inside and out, his or her every thought and motivation, while we can only guess and wonder. I know; I tried to figure Larry out for many years. Just when I thought I had done it, I discovered I was wrong!

In fact, our interference hampers God. When I first heard that, I thought, *Humphf! Well, excuse me! I was only trying to help.* Unfortunately, our "help" is not help at all. It's a hindrance. God can—and wants to—do it alone. But he does delegate to us an important job: to love and accept our spouse! Then he'll do whatever else is necessary. Unfortunately, we think our anger can change them, but it only makes them more determined to have their own way. Dr. Neil Anderson, author of *The Bondage Breaker,* says, "When you seek to play the role of the Holy Spirit in another person's life, you will misdirect that person's battle with God onto yourself."

Claim God's promise of sovereign control: "The king's heart is like channels of water in the hand of the Lord; He turns it wherever He wishes" (Proverbs 21:1). If God can change the hearts of kings, then he can certainly change our hearts and the heart of our spouse.

Because God wants us to have a happy marriage, we can trust him to do what is best, and we can love our spouse by faith. Proverbs 3:4-6 says, "If you want favor with both God and man [your mate], and a reputation for good judgment and common sense, then trust the Lord completely; don't ever trust yourself. In everything you do, put God first, and he will direct you and crown your efforts with success [a happy, godly marriage]" (TLB) (added information mine).

As we allow God to work in our marriage, it is comforting to remember that we most often get angry with the people who mean the most to us. Sharing our angry *feelings,* not attitudes or actions, reflects that love. It tells our spouse, "I respect you enough to want to share this part of myself with you. Doing this shows my commitment to our relationship." But we need to be careful to share with "I feel" messages, rather than saying, "You are . . ." or "You make me . . ." (We'll discuss how to do this in more detail in chapter 7.)

In the past, watching the Lord work in my husband's life—in what I sometimes judged to be impotent ways—made me think at times that God didn't know what he was doing, and that he would never get Larry to come around. But God performed miracles, and now I rejoice in our beautiful, rich life together. Just recently we celebrated our twenty-fifth wedding anniversary. God has also given us the joy and privilege of speaking together at couples' seminars and retreats. We both marvel at what God has done.

When we were in that pit of discontentment, we never thought we'd make it this far. Not only have we made it, we're rejoicing in our relationship. And it's our biggest thrill to be able to share with others how they also can strengthen and, if necessary, heal their relationships.

Submission and Responsibility

The Bible says in Ephesians 5:21 that we are to submit to each other in Christ. I strongly believe in the principle of allowing God to work in our spouse's life, but that doesn't mean we become doormats to be walked on. True submission means we are to offer to our spouse who we are, what we believe, what we would like, etc. Then we can leave the results to the Lord, and not get so angry trying to change things.

Luci and her family of six lived in a small apartment. She was angry with her husband about his unhappiness with their small place. She wrote to me, "He's the major cause of my discomfort. He's so disillusioned that he is incapable of giving me any encouragement. He's so tired of our apartment that he stays away from here as much as possible, which isn't very much fun for me. I try to do my best, but it doesn't seem to be good enough. I'm feeling angry because of his feelings toward our outgrown home."

Luci gathered her courage and shared her feelings with her husband. She filled me in: "We talked a bit, and he reassured me that his disappointment is not a reflection on me as a homemaker, but rather a reflection of our financial pressures."

She had declared her feelings—submitted to her husband who she was at that moment—and she felt better because of it. The financial problems weren't gone, but she no longer needed to take her tension and anger out on her children.

A related cause of anger with our spouses is *when we take on personal responsibility for his or her responses or behavior.* I am not responsible for Larry's reactions or behavior. I am responsible *to* him, in the sense that I need to be the wife that God wants me to be. But I am not accountable for Larry.

My friend Debra shared with me that she and her husband traveled into Los Angeles one day to take their kids to the zoo. After spending the day there, they left a little later than they'd wanted and were stuck in traffic on the way home. Debra started feeling tense, afraid that her husband would be angry. Then she realized that she was taking responsibility for her husband's reaction. She consciously relaxed and decided she couldn't change his attitude even if he were upset (which, it turned out, he wasn't). Debra's choice showed her growing self-esteem and ability to identify the causes of potential anger.

Help for Single Parents

We've talked about the relationship between our spouses and our anger, but what about those who are now single parents, either by divorce, death, or choice? If you are divorced, you may not have wanted the divorce, or you may have needed to get out of an abusive marriage. While I rejoice in my healed marriage relationship, I recognize that it doesn't always turn out like that, even when one partner sincerely hopes and works and prays hard toward that end. I have talked with many single parents who wanted their marriage to work, yet it didn't.

Dealing with an ex-spouse is often difficult and frustrating and anger-inducing. You may be concerned about your ex-mate's poor influence upon your children as they spend time with him or her. You may feel abandoned and discouraged because life seems out of control.

Or you may feel lonely and devastated after your spouse's death. Maybe you even wonder if he died on purpose. It seems like a silly thought, but when we don't have someone special to build us up, we start taking everything personally and get frustrated as a result.

Are you single by choice, and are now doubting if it was the best idea? Maybe you wonder how God can help you raise well-adjusted children when you can't be both mother and father to them.

Whatever your situation, God knows about you and your children. He wants to help you deal with whatever anger your situation has caused. God loves you and cares. He wants to make a difference, and he will protect your children.

Continue to do the best you can. Seek the help of others. Don't try to be a "Lone Ranger" parent who never gets assistance through babysitting. You need time for fun and to be alone. Twenty-four-hour days with your children or spending every moment with them after work is not what they, or you, really need—especially when it creates greater stress and frustration in you. Find ways to get other people involved in your parenting, and get some time for yourself. You'll be a better parent because of it.

Parenting is always a challenge, whether or not we have a spouse to support us. We'll be able to cope with our normal frustrations better when we allow God to work in our spouse's lives instead of believing we can control and change them. Let's look now at some steps we can take for constructively dealing with anger. There is hope!

7

Defusing the Anger Bomb

Now that we've examined what anger is and some of its many causes, you may be thinking, *Well, that's good information, but can I really change and control my anger?* With God's help, yes, you can. Let's look at a constructive five-step method of defusing anger that has worked for me.

Our goal is to have healthy and appropriate reactions to stressful situations. By going through this process every time you get angry, you will become more aware of your feelings, and be able to possess and own them (as opposed to your feelings possessing and controlling you).

1. Realize that you feel angry.
Elaine has been a Christian for four years and condemns herself for the way she reacts toward her five-year-old son. When I asked her to describe her anger, she used strong terms, such as "rage," "heat," "out of control." Then I asked her how she feels before she loses her temper. She replied, "I feel calm, and then I suddenly blow up."

I explained to her that she had repressed and ignored her first feelings of anger for so long that she could no longer identify them in the early stages. I encouraged her to begin paying attention to her early warning signals before she blew up, and to realize and admit that she feels angry.

Recognizing early signs of anger—your "red-flag warnings"—gives you time to deal with your feelings before they become destructive. To discover these signals, write down facts about the last three times you blew it. Then recall how you felt fifteen minutes, ten minutes, and five minutes before the flare-ups. If you can't remember those details, then monitor the next three times it happens. Chances are, you'll see a pattern of warnings in the three incidents.

For instance, fifteen minutes before I blow up, I usually am worried about staying on a time schedule or some other pressure. At the ten-minute warning I feel tense and hurried. Even though on the outside I may not look hassled, inside I feel like the wheels are turning faster than normal. My five-minute signal is that I'm gritting and grinding my teeth and raising my voice in quick, terse commands.

I've heard a variety of examples of these "red-flag warnings" at many parenting seminars and classes I've conducted. People report they feel hot, cold, paralyzed, tightened muscles, a churning stomach, a desire to cry, and other reactions. We are each unique in the way we respond to anger.

When I share these ideas with fathers, they are primarily the ones who don't have a sense of their early warning signals. Like Elaine, they aren't in tune with their feelings and think of themselves as calm until they blow up. When they are attending a longer, weekly class, I can tell them to watch for their warning signs the next week. Every single time, they return and report their amazement that they did have signals after all; they just hadn't connected those reactions to their anger. If your spouse is unaware of his or her feelings, gently point out the warning signs you have noticed—*after* he or she calms down! Pointing them out while your spouse is in the heat of the anger may only fuel that anger.

When you become aware of your unique red-flag warnings, you realize that your fifteen-minute countdown to explosion has started. At this point, you can break the cycle.

2. Magnetize your mind away from the anger.

The second step to defusing your anger is to magnetize your mind away from your anger by using what I call a *distractor.* A distractor is anything that takes your mind off your anger, if only for a few minutes. This gives you a break to cool down. Remember how we said earlier that anger always causes physical tension and energy? A distractor helps to relieve that tension before you blow up at another person or take it out in a destructive, physical way. This step is not the solution for our anger, but it is an important one.

Being distracted for a few minutes allows us to come back to the situation with an improved, calmer perspective. Like steam from a whistling kettle, the steam of our anger is released. The cause of the anger is still there (that's taken care of in step 3), but at least the energy that makes us want to lash out is gone.

Here are a few possible distractors:

- Take a vigorous walk.
- Run in place.
- Hit a pillow or a punching bag.
- Take a shower (with or without screaming).
- Sing loudly.
- Take ten slow, deep breaths; count them out loud.
- Play a musical instrument.
- Recite an uplifting Bible verse.
- Telephone a friend, a hotline, or a professional counselor.
- Watch a funny television show.

At one of my parenting seminars, someone spoke up and said, "I know, I'll throw marshmallows when I'm feeling angry." I thought that was a great idea—intense, but safe! Within ten seconds, though, someone else spoke up and said, "No, that wouldn't work for me. I want to destroy something." Everyone laughed. I think it was because they related!

The important part of this exercise is to determine our distracting action *beforehand,* when we're not angry, practice it, and ask God to remind us to use it when we feel the anger bomb building.

For instance, during a peaceful period, I tell myself that the next time I feel angry, I'll take three steps backward and walk away from the irritating or frustrating situation. I continue to remind myself and rehearse it in my mind. I may even take three steps backward once in a while to practice. Then, when I notice I'm getting within my fifteen- or ten-minute countdown range, I remember, *Aha! It's time for me to take three steps backward and walk away!* That gives me time to think through what's causing my anger and how I can resolve it.

Deep breathing is another simple distractor that I have found helpful. It's especially effective because intense emotions inhibit breathing. As I get angry, my chest muscles seem to tighten and tense up. Slow, deep breathing eliminates that pressure.

A third distractor that worked well for me was to separate myself from my children and jog in place. By furiously jogging in place, sometimes for what seemed like five minutes but was more likely one minute, I expended potentially hurtful energy. When I think of how I did that, I smile because I must have looked quite silly. But it worked!

A friend shared her distractor with me. When her baby was screaming and her toddler wouldn't cooperate by going to sleep, she called a friend. After they talked briefly, her friend asked to speak to the toddler. The friend told her a bedtime story and sang a lullaby over the phone, then the little girl cheerfully went off to bed. That was a distractor for both the mother and the child!

Several of these ideas for distracting ourselves require that we take time for a quick break, but that can be difficult because we're often rushing around from being late for an appointment or meeting. At those times we must convince ourselves that going through these steps is more important than being on time or accomplishing the task before us. If we'll risk being late or having less time for reaching our goal, in the long run we'll be less angry—and that's even more valuable than being on time.

Once we do distract ourselves and cool down, we are more able to go on to the third step and think more clearly.

3. Recognize the underlying cause of your anger.
As we discussed earlier, in most cases, the immediate circumstances are not the real cause of our anger. Instead, we may be displacing our anger from the real cause, and transferring an emotion to a logically inappropriate object.

I find it helpful to keep a mental checklist of possible causes, which I quickly go through to try to determine the actual cause. Here are the questions I use, broken down into three categories. You may want to use these and add your own.

- *Physical:* Am I tired? Do I need some exercise? Have I been eating too much sugar? Am I in a premenstrual depression?
- *Psychological:* Am I thinking negatively about something? Am I worried? Is a relationship troubling me? Are

my expectations for myself, my child, or someone else unrealistic? Am I feeling embarrassed, frustrated, or insecure about something? Is my self-esteem low? Have my goals or desires been blocked? Has my child mirrored a bad habit of mine?

- *Spiritual:* Am I not trusting God? Do I have some unconfessed sin? Is there someone I need to forgive? Am I bitter toward someone or God?

It is important to dig up the underlying cause and expose it. Then we can recognize that whatever is going wrong probably doesn't warrant the kind of intense reaction and behavior that's building within us.

4. Analyze your thinking for incorrect assumptions.
Many times we become angry because we assume an idea is true when it is not. Then we react based on that incorrect assumption. For instance, I may become easily angered at my husband because I believe he is responsible for meeting my needs. I must combat that wrong assumption with the truth that only God can meet my needs completely.

Here are some other wrong assumptions that I and others have found within our thinking:

- Being financially secure will take away all my problems.
- My spouse should know instinctively what's important to me.
- My children are a reflection of me.
- Anger is an effective disciplinary tool.
- I can control my child.
- I have a right to have time to myself; therefore, the children must take a nap.

These underlying assumptions warp our thinking, yet we believe we're basing our attitudes and actions on truth. Stopping to evaluate our thinking by examining Scripture and by sharing our ideas with others will help us to identify wrong ideas. Once we do, anger won't have as much fuel to feed it. Then we can travel to the fifth and final step.

5. Verbalize your anger appropriately.

As Christians, we are exhorted in Scripture to speak "the truth in love" (Ephesians 4:15). Here are a few helpful ways to begin communicating more lovingly when we are overcome with anger.

Use "I" messages instead of "you" messages. "You" messages express blame: "You make me angry," "You shouldn't do that." As a result, the other person usually responds defensively and is not open to hearing your feelings or ideas for a solution to the problem.

On the other hand, "I" messages express how you feel, without telling the other person what to do about it (unless he or she asks). "I am really upset and hurt," "I feel very frustrated right now," express your needs and may be more conducive to someone really listening to you.

In addition to watching the wording, you need to monitor your motives. Don't use "I" messages to try to subtly change the other person. Instead, honestly share your feelings, while trusting God to control your circumstances.

Note that these "I" messages are primarily designed to be used with adults rather than with our children. (If you haven't noticed, children aren't usually motivated by our needs.) Although we can share our feelings with them, motivating them will be more successful by establishing rules and then following through with consequences if they break them.

Here are some examples of how you can change "you" statements into more useful "I feel" statements:

"You" Messages	TO	"I" Messages

"You never pay the bills."

"I feel tense when the bills get stacked up unpaid. But I feel relieved when they're paid right away. My expectation is that they would get paid soon. What is your expectation?"

"You are never home."

"I feel lonely when I spend so much time by myself. But I feel excited when I'm included in activities with you. My expectation is that we would spend a lot of time together. What is your expectation?"

"When you don't do what I say, I feel that you aren't supporting me."

"I feel discouraged when my desires aren't considered important. But I feel secure when my opinions are listened to. My expectation is that we would communicate fully before a decision is made. What is your expectation?"

(With the above "you" message, did you notice the "I feel" was included? Even so, it was not a true "I feel" message because "you" was still a part of it.)

"If you don't go to church
with me, I'm not going to
that sporting event with you."

"I feel sad when I go to
church alone. But I feel
thrilled when the kids see a
wise choice being made. My
expectation is that we would
make church a priority. What
is your expectation?"

Look at the four steps involved. First we state the unpleasant
feeling we have when our expectation isn't met. Then we share
the pleasant feeling we have when it is met. Third, we state
our expectation, and finally ask for input on the other person's
expectation. Sharing such "I" messages won't solve all our
problems, but it can lay the foundation for good communication so that the problem can be resolved.

Another way to verbalize our anger is to call a friend who
will keep a confidence and not put us down for our emotions.
Another possibility is to call a hotline, a professional counselor, or our pastor.

It is most effective to express our feelings *at the time of
the misunderstanding.* If we can't seem to talk about them at
that moment, though, we might try preparing ourselves for
verbalizing our feelings later by writing them out. A woman
shared this insight with me and said it works for her.

When she realizes that she is angry with someone, whether
it is her husband, a neighbor, or a friend, she first determines
what really is bothering her, and then she writes down her
feelings and the explanation she wants to give them. By doing
so, she can ensure that she expresses her feelings in a way
the other person can accept. Then she reads it to someone
else, who can help her critique it. Finally, she practices it before she actually calls or visits the person involved. This process gives her the courage she needs to confront the person,

because she knows she's expressing herself in the best possible way.

Another aspect of verbalizing our anger appropriately involves *taking responsibility for our reactions.* No one makes me angry; it is my choice. Once I am accountable for my own response, I need to express my feelings appropriately and ask forgiveness for my part of the problem. Whether or not the other person accepts my apology or changes his mind or actions, I can choose healthy reactions and try not to control the other person. I can trust God to work in both of our lives.

When we do need to confront others, here are some guidelines to follow:

- Pick a good time and place, with the least distractions.
- Have good motives; desire the best for the other person, not their hurt.
- Give up expectations of a particular response.
- Be willing to forgive.
- Prepare what you'll say; write it out, practice it.
- Be firm, but avoid name calling or screaming.
- Admit your wrongdoing.
- Stay on the issue; don't exaggerate or threaten.
- Don't use absolute words and phrases like *never, always, all the time, every day, constantly.*

As you look over that list, which principle is easiest for you to follow, and which one might be the most difficult? It's good to give ourselves credit for what we do well and be aware of where we can improve.

Putting the Five Steps into Action

Recently I applied these principles when a woman broke a promise to me and I felt deeply hurt. After the initial hurt, the anger came. I knew I would have to travel through my five-step process so that I wouldn't take my anger out on my children.

I realized that I was indeed angry. Even after I tried to understand my friend's viewpoint, I still believed that she had treated me inappropriately.

Then I played the piano for a while to pound out some of the energy that my anger was creating. That was my distractor.

Finding the real cause of my anger was obvious to me. Yet when I thought more about the situation, I discovered even more reasons why I was angry. For instance, her broken promise prevented me from completing a project I'd promised for someone else. Therefore, not only was I angry because of how she had treated me, but I was also angry because it influenced my reputation before others.

In analyzing my thinking for incorrect assumptions, I realized that what I had regarded as her promise, she had actually intended as a possibility. I had assumed we were communicating at the same level, and I learned that I needed to be more assertive in determining the position of someone else's plans and thinking.

Finally, I verbalized my anger in a letter to her. I really let my fury fly. Then I edited it to make my sharing appropriate and acceptable. In the letter, I asked her to forgive me for my reactions and I shared how she had hurt me. Larry read my edited letter and approved it. As I typed the final letter, I decided to wait one week before I mailed it, to make sure that the Lord wanted me to send it.

The next day my anger was gone. I knew I wouldn't mail that letter. "Verbalizing" my anger, even on paper, had dissolved it, and I was able to forgive her. Today I have no bitterness toward her.

By traveling through that five-step process, I worked through my anger in a healthy way, preventing any displaced anger from spilling onto my children. I encourage you to travel through those same steps. Write out the steps on cards, and place them throughout your home—even carry one in your purse or pocket. Then when you notice your "red-flag warnings," you can quickly refer to the list and go through them. I've seen it make a difference in me, and I know the Lord will help you with it also.

Finding Spiritual Strength

Another source of help for handling our anger is a relationship with God through his Son, Jesus Christ. Being a Christian does not mean we'll be perfect or have an anger-free life, but it does mean we'll have God's power available to us to help us overcome our difficulties. Philippians 4:13 says, "I can do all things through Christ, who strengthens me."

Taking time to pray and study the Bible are at the source of that strength. Unfortunately, these disciplines are not very compatible with raising children because of the time caring for children can take. It happened to me, and I've heard many parents report the same; even if they try to wake up early to have a "quiet time," the children wake up early too. So it's a dilemma.

If we are perfectionistic, we may just give up, thinking that if we can't spend a full hour alone with the Lord, we might as well not try at all. That kind of all-or-nothing attitude can be Satan's lie to discourage any time with God.

Instead, think "small yet valuable." One woman in my parenting class said how she "tithes" her alone time. If she anticipates her children taking a two-hour nap, she takes 10 percent of that time and spends it with the Lord. Twelve minutes might not seem like much, but I believe God is pleased with whatever time we give him. He understands our busy lives and the demands of our children. If we concentrate on him for whatever time we can, he'll be there.

Some other possibilities are to have a devotional book in the bathroom—most likely the only room in your house you can lock yourself in! Of course the children will still be outside the door, pounding away and calling for you, but at least you can concentrate for a few seconds on your devotional book. God will honor whatever efforts we make. Our spiritual "plant" will be fed and then be strengthened to weather the hot winds of parenting. Don't give up trying to find the devotional time you need.

If this "spiritual talk" seems rather strange to you because you've never experienced a relationship with God, I encourage you to consider your need of forgiveness and cleansing. Jesus died on the cross for you, and rose again from the dead, wanting to make you his friend and child. If you would like to make a decision to follow Jesus right now, please pray this prayer and share your own desires with God:

"Heavenly Father, thank you for sending Jesus to die for me. I realize that I need your forgiveness and cleansing. I want to become your child. Please come into my life and make me a new creature in Christ. I love you and want to learn to love you more. Amen."

God wants to honor your prayer because he wants to be involved in your life. Even if you don't feel different, you can take God at his word. Consider these verses from the Bible:

> God has given us eternal life, and this life is in His Son. He who has the Son has the life; he who does not have the Son of God does not have the life. These things I have written to you who believe in the name of the Son of God, in order that you may know that you have eternal life." (1 John 5:11-13)

Notice it says, "so that you may *know.*" Not *wish* or *hope,* but *know!* God wants you to be assured of his love and the gift of salvation you've now received. He is a source of help and grace as we learn how to defuse our anger in new ways.

8

There Is Hope!

James S. Stewart said, "The very disillusionment of today is the raw material of the Christian hope." That certainly applies to parenting, especially when we're disillusioned about our angry responses to our children. But with God, nothing is impossible—there is always hope.

Even as I was preparing to write this chapter, I got a phone call from Margie. I had first met Margie when I spoke at a women's luncheon at her church. She came up afterward and poured out her heart and concern about being angry with her four-year-old daughter, Melissa. "Will I ever become the loving, patient mother I want to be?" she asked with tears in her eyes. We talked about some practical steps she could take and then I prayed for her. She called me a few times after that, usually when she was overwhelmed with being a mom.

But today's call was one of victory. It's been three years now and she jubilantly said, "I just had to tell you we're moving out of state and I'm going as a mother who is in control of her anger. I'm not perfect, but I know I'm farther on the road of being the patient parent I'd wanted to be. Your prayer for me was the first step, and since then God has done a number of healing things. Thank you."

At that point of fear three years ago, Margie believed her anger and poor reactions would create problems in her daughter in the future. Such fear is common in those of us who wonder what our anger will do to our children. Certainly we must do everything we can to improve our parenting skills and learn, but fear over the future will only paralyze our minds from responding now in the best possible way.

God tells us, "Be anxious for nothing, but in everything by prayer and supplication with thanksgiving, let your requests be made known to God" (Philippians 4:6). That "nothing" includes our children's future. Worry doesn't make our children good adults. But asking for God's help and guidance right now will.

As an abusive mother who was paralyzed with that kind of fear, I was convinced my anger would cause permanent wounds deep in Darcy's emotional being. As God did his healing work, my worry subsided. Then when Darcy was in third grade, something happened that seemed to almost wipe it out completely.

At that time, my first book had just been published, which told the story of how I'd overcome being an abusive mother. Darcy was so excited about its publication that she said, "Mom, I want to take your book to school and show it to my teacher." *What?* I thought. *Oh, sure, I want everyone to know you were abused.* But I had begun sharing my story with groups, so there wasn't any reason Darcy shouldn't share it too.

She took the book to school and I heard that not only her teacher, but several of the teachers and principal at her public school also read it. Several months later, Darcy returned home from school with the book in hand. Attached to the book was a note from her teacher that read, "I really love your daughter. She's a healthy, well adjusted little girl."

I stood there staring at that note as if it were a note from God himself. Darcy wasn't ruined for life. God had healed her. Why was I worrying when other people could see it too?

I soon found one of God's promises in Joel 2:25-26 that increased my hope and diminished my worry even more:

> Then I will make up to you for the years that the swarming locust has eaten, the creeping locust, the stripping locust, and the gnawing locust, my great army which I sent among you. And you shall have plenty to eat and be satisfied, and praise the name of the Lord your God, who has dealt wondrously with you; then My people will never be put to shame.

My own paraphrase of this passage goes like this:

> Then I will make up to you for the years you yelled at your children, or spanked them in anger, or even abused them. And you shall become a loving parent and be pleased with your parental reactions. As a result, you will give me glory and honor, and even other people will credit me with the changes in your home.

With God, There Is Always Hope

For many years I qualified the hope offered in Romans 8:28: "And we know that God causes all things to work together for good to those who love God, to those who are called according to His purpose." I usually added, "And we know that God causes all things, *except child abuse,* to work together for good . . ." I found it hard to believe that God could use something as bad as child abuse for good.

Yet that's exactly what he has done. There are no exceptions to that promise. I now have the privilege of sharing hope with others because of God's power in delivering me. If God had given me the instantaneous deliverance from my anger for which I kept asking, I wouldn't have learned the things I needed to know. But because he took me through that process of growth and learning, I have valuable lessons to share. When I was in that pit of anger, I couldn't imagine sharing anything with anybody. I couldn't even see out of the dark hole! But God knew exactly how he would use the pain in my life for good, and he deserves all the praise and glory.

Today, my daughter is a beautiful, twenty-one-year-old college senior. She's thinking of becoming a Secret Service agent after graduation. We have a good relationship, one that I would have never thought possible because of the way I treated her. She often shares my books with her friends, and we can talk about what happened.

She has forgiven me and freely tells me, "I love you, Mom." Those are the best words I could possibly hear from her, words I feared I would never hear. Even as I write, tears come to my eyes because it means so much to me. How grateful I am that with God there is always hope.

Are you lacking hope today? Do you feel that you will never be able to defuse your anger? Then claim God's promise in Jeremiah 29:11: "'For I know the plans that I have for you,' declares the Lord, 'plans for welfare and not for calamity to give you a future and a hope.' "

Even though your journey out of the pit of anger may seem agonizingly slow, take heart. God knows exactly how he's going to bring you through it. Just keep trusting in him. And if you fail, as we all do, then receive his forgiveness and take a fresh hold of his strength. He is the God of second chances. He'll never give up on you.

To the Reader

If you took a step of faith, or would like to write me for any reason, I would be delighted to hear from you. My address is:

Kathy Collard Miller
P.O. Box 1058
Placentia, CA 92670

Notes

Chapter 3: What Is Anger?

1. David Augsburger, *Be All You Can Be* (Carol Stream, Ill.: Creation House, 1970), p. 60.

2. Theodore Isaac Rubin, *The Angry Book* (New York: MacMillan Company, 1969), pp. 130–31.

3. John Powell, *Why Am I Afraid to Tell You Who I Am?* (Niles, Ill: Argus Communications, 1969), p. 155.

4. H. Norman Wright, *Communication: Key to Your Marriage* (Glendale, Calif.: Regal Books, 1974), p. 91.

Chapter 4: The Myth of Perfection

1. David Seamands, *Healing for Damaged Emotions* (Wheaton, Ill: Victor Books, 1984), p. 78.